Pocket Guide to

Flags

Pocket Guide to

Flags

Sue Heady

G^E

This edition published 2001 by

PRC Publishing Ltd,

a subsidiary of Chrysalis Books

Kiln House, 210 New Kings Road, London SW6 4NZ

Produced for Greenwich Editions

10, Blenheim Court, Brewery Road

London, N7 9NT

ISBN 0 86288 432 2

Printed and bound in China

CONTENTS

PART ONE

INTRODUCTION

Flags are amazing things. They play such an important part in daily life—for example, in national, political, and sporting arenas—and yet most people know very little about them.

We may know the history of the Union Jack and the Stars and Stripes, probably the two most famous flags in the world, plus that of our own national flag (if it differs from these two). We probably all know that a white flag signals a truce and could identify the United Nations flag if it was put in front of us. But how many of us could explain the symbolism of the colors used and name the various parts that constitute a flag? Probably very few. In other words, our general knowledge of flags is actually very limited.

This is a shame, because the flag—being so visible from great distances—is probably the oldest form of communication known to man. Since time immemorial, he has felt the need to use a staff or vexillum (the precursors to the flag) and, subsequently, a flag to distinguish himself, his family, and his country. In fact, there's so much to learn about all aspects of the flag that the term "vexillology" (from the Latin word *vexillum* meaning banner, which in turn is derived from the word *velum* meaning sail) has been coined to cover "the study and collection of information about flags."

The purpose of this book, then, is to introduce the reader to the basics of vexillology. In doing so, I have started with a chapter that explains all the flag essentials and terminology associated with vexillology. The second chapter follows the development of flags since they were first used by ancient civilizations, and the third the history of sea flags. The fourth and final chapter provides details of the histories and symbolism associated with some of the key flags in use around the world today. Finally, there is a gazetteer featuring the flag of every country in the world, alongside some useful snippets of national information.

I hope you enjoy the book and that you obtain many fascinating insights into the world of flags from it—I certainly have while I've been researching it. Happy reading!

The American flag at Tranquility Base on the Moon, planted by the Apollo 11 astronauts.

FLAGS: THE BASICS

A flag fluttering gently in the wind seems such a simple object: it's just a piece of colored cloth attached to a flagpole, right? Well, actually, no, it's not quite that straightforward. Some very precise terminology exists to describe the various elements of a flag and so, before proceeding to the history of flags in general and flags of particular interest, this chapter explains the jargon.

There are many kinds of flag and each differs in some way, be it on account of its shape, design, color, proportions, material, and/or accessories. One factor that is always constant, however, is that flags officially fly from left to right—the exception to the rule being flags of Arabic nations and those whose language is written from right to left. So, in all the descriptions that follow, it is assumed that the flag is flying to the right of a vertical flagpole. This "front" side of the flag is known as the obverse, while the other side is the reverse. The latter is usually a mirror image of the obverse, but there are a few flags—most of which are military—that have two different sides and are, effectively, two flags sewn back to back.

Flag Shapes

Asked to think of a flag, one that is rectangular in shape (such as the Union Jack) will almost certainly spring to mind. Certainly, rectangular flags are standard these days and most of the modern flags flown on land and sea are this shape, but—at a push—you will probably be able to recall seeing a few squarish flags at military parades (or the black and white checked variety at the end of a Formula One race) and triangular "bunting" at parties. Flags have not always been so uniform in appearance: in the Middle Ages, they came in a variety of shapes.

14th century painting showing early triangular flags attached to lances.

One of the earliest flags in general usage was a *gonfanon*, a flag with three or more tails. In use from the beginning of the ninth century, its use was initially reserved for rulers, but after the 11th century, it prevailed in the army and from the 12th to the 14th centuries was used by cities. In the 15th century, the banner gradually replaced it. The *pavon*, an early form of the pennon (details of which follow), was triangular and attached to a lance by one of the long sides, with the narrow pointed end at the top. Being unsuited to anything but the simplest of arms, the pavon was soon replaced by the *pennon*, which was similar in shape but larger. Pennons were carried by knights, while bannerets (knights who were entitled to command other knights), barons, viscounts, counts, and marquises had banners; kings had both. (On being created a banneret, the tail of a knight's pennon was cut off to reduce it down to a banner shape.) As you can imagine, all these flags could confuse esquires on the battlefield, because they might be able to remember what the pennon of their knight looked like (as well as those of their nearest neighbors), but they could not be expected to recall those of all the knights fighting on their side. So King Richard II of England (1367–1400) decided that all pennons should just bear royal arms and, from the second half of the 14th century, this trend spread across Europe.

The *banner*, which replaced the gonfanon in general use, is the easiest flag to define because it was usually rectangular—the same shape as most modern flags. The first banners, however, were "upright" rectangles, which means they were much deeper than they were wide. There was a practical reason for this: the deep, narrow shape did not interfere in the handling of an esquire's lance. There was also a square banner and what was known as an extended banner,

The choir banners at St. Patrick's Cathedral in Dublin, Ireland.

because it was longer rather than deeper—in other words, exactly the same shape as today's Union Jack. Whatever shape they took, banners usually bore the arms of a titled person. Think, for example, of the "Royal Standard" (the correct name of which is the "Royal Banner").

The *schwenkel*—well known in Germanic usage—is a long strip of material that was added to the upper corner of a banner furthest from the flagpole and was generally carried by those of higher rank. In usage by the 14th century, it is thought to have been adopted purely on decorative grounds.

During the 15th century, martial flags became longer and narrower.

The *standard*, a word in use by around 1230, was an elongated flag that probably originated in England and made its appearance in France toward the end of the 14th century. Until well into the 15th century, it was either swallow-tailed (deeply split, with pointed tails), fork-tailed (less deeply split), or ended in a single sharp point. Early standards carried the arms of the titled, but later versions featured the cross of St. George in England and that of St. Andrew in Scotland.

The *guidon*, a long and narrow flag ending either in a blunt or pointed end, was originally considered a flag for archers and, for that reason, was never folded in war, because it was used to lead and rally the archers. The term guidon is derived from the French word "guide-homme" (which roughly translates as "something that guides a man"), and was first used by Anglo-Burgundian forces in 1492. Always a military flag, the flags used by certain British cavalry regiments today are still called guidons. Similar to the flags of old, they measure around a meter in length and 70 centimeters in depth, and have a slit with rounded corners.

The *cornet*, a long, narrow oblong flag, was a larger version of the banderole that was worn on the helmet. It was primarily used by groups of cavalry and artillery that were too small to carry a guidon or standard, as it was less of a disgrace to lose a smaller flag. The *streamer*, which usually ended in a single point, was placed

Streamers flying on an English ship.

at the top of a castle or ship, and could measure up to 60 meters. For example, the Earl of Warwick had a streamer made in 1437 that measured roughly eight meters by 40 meters, and bore both the cross of St. George and his own arms. Streamers went out of fashion in the 17th century and were replaced with the

Fish-shaped windsocks are raised on a pole to celebrate a boys festival in Kyoto, Japan.

pennant, a smaller version of the streamer.

Most of these flags are no longer in common usage, although you are still quite likely to see them flying at historical sites or, of course, during the reconstruction of famous battles that have become popular weekend activities in recent years. However, there is one unusual ancient flag that is still in wide usage these days and that is the Japanese *windsock*, a truncated cone of textile mounted on a mast so that it is free to rotate about a vertical axis, which is used at airports to gauge wind direction.

Flags currently used at sea tend to be a law unto themselves. To start with, while the word "flag" applies to flags flown on land and sea, flags flown at sea can also be called ensigns. Why they should have a different name remains something of a mystery, but it is perhaps not that surprising given that other European languages, including French, have two separate words to distinguish between those on land and sea: a French ship flies "pavillons," while flags flown on land are known as "drapeaux."

As we learned earlier, both streamers and pennants have been used on land, as well as at sea. In 1514, for example, Henry VIII commissioned a streamer for his fleet that was the largest flag ever flown by the British navy: it measured roughly 50 meters in length. In fact, the most common type of sea flag has always been a *pennant*. Today, a ship has the potential to fly a masthead pennant (the mark of a naval vessel in commission), which is long and narrow; the broad, swallow-tailed pennant of a naval commodore; and the blunt-ended pennants of the International Code of Signals. The *flag of command* is hoisted instead of a masthead pennant when the flag officer, rank of read admiral or above, is aboard.

The *ensign*, which is traditionally found at the stern and is rectangular in shape, is the principal identifying national flag of warships and merchant ships. On sailing ships, the civil ensign is often displayed from a halyard attached to the mizzenmast. Yachts fly the civil ensign on the stern and a triangular club *burgee* or private flag on the mast.

One of the oldest flags in use on ships is the *jack*, which is normally a smaller rectangle than the ensign and is flown from a jack staff at the bows of the ship. In strict usage, the term "Union Jack" should only be used to describe the small version of the Union Flag seen at the bow of a Royal Navy ship, but it has been assimilated into common usage for many years now . And it is only found on Royal Navy ships, because they are the only vessels allowed to use the Union Jack and Union Flag, according to a parliamentary act dating to 1634. (On land, of course, the Union Flag is the national flag of the United Kingdom and may be used by anyone.)

Since the 19th century, merchant ships owned by a company or individual have also flown a *house flag*, usually rectangular, which carries the company's or individual's personal colors or emblem on the foremast.

Flag Design

A flag may look like a rectangular piece of material, but vexillologists divide it into sections, each with its own name. The whole of the flag is known as the *field*. The field is then broken down into four quarters. Looking at the obverse side of a flag, the upper left hand quarter is called the *upper* (or *top*) *hoist*, while the lower left-hand quarter is the *lower* (or *bottom*) hoist; together, they are known as the *first half*. Meanwhile, the upper right hand quarter is called the *upper* (or *top*) *fly* and the lower right hand quarter is the *lower* (or *bottom*) *fly*; together, they form the second half of the flag. A cross, such as the St. George in the English flag, often divides a flag neatly into its quarters. The upper hoist is also known as the *canton* and is often used for a coat of arms or emblem. For example, the stars in the United States flag are located in the canton. A flag can also be divided into four by a *saltire*

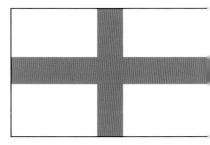

The neatly quartered flag of England—the St. George Cross.

(or diagonal cross). The colors of the triangles that result from a division by saltire are given clockwise, beginning with the triangle that is entirely within the first half of the flag. The middle of the flag is known as the *centre* and is where— if one is used—a crest is usually placed.

A crest and any number of design devices that are placed in the field of a flag are known as *charges*. If used, they should be large and as simple as possible, and should be placed in the most important parts of the field (in other words, the

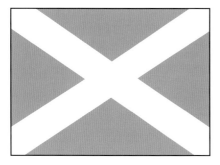

Scotland's flag—the St. Andrew Cross—a typical saltire design.

canton or centre), so that they can be "read" when a flag is seen from a distance or fluttering in the wind. Some of the most popular charges on modern flags are cantons (which can be either oblong or—less often—square), stars, crosses and triangles. Some charges, like the canton, often carry another charge, such as stars (in the case of the American Stars and Stripes) or a coat of arms. Bends and crosses can be "fimbriated;" in other words, edged with narrow stripes. Charges are often used to express an idea that would otherwise take a lot of words to explain. In medieval times, for example, some of the most popular charges were crosses (representing Christianity) and lions (representing both kingship and bravery). Today, and ever since the American Revolution in 1777, when they came to be used to represent the states of the Union, stars are popular charges—they currently appear on more than 50 national flags.

One very noticeable development in flag design over the centuries has been the change from the really quite ornate to the very simple. While medieval flags featured coats of arms that were often painted or embroidered on to material, most modern flags are simple color divisions of the field with, maybe, the odd simple charge. These divisions tend to be chosen not only for aesthetic reasons, but also to enhance the flag's symbolic meaning—as explained in the Flag Color section, the different colored stripes can represent different ideas.

The division of the field using horizontal or vertical lines results in horizontal or vertical stripes, while dividing the field diagonally creates "bends." Generally, these division lines are straight, but in the design of some national, provincial, and civic flags, wavy and serrated lines are used. If the lines are of equal width, then only their number is given in the flag's written description, but if a design consists of stripes or bends of unequal size, the proportions are quoted. For example, the flag of Thailand features five horizontal stripes, which are in the following proportions 1:1:2:1:1, which means that the middle stripe is twice as wide as each of the outer stripes. For the same reason, so as to be easily recognizable from great distances, sea flags are also of simple design.

These are the very basic rules of flag design. If followed, the end result should be a flag that is straightforward, yet distinctive and meaningful, because—ultimately—a flag is a medium of communication and its message should, therefore, be easy to recognize.

Flag Color

Color is very important in flag design, because it can convey a great deal of symbolic meaning that may imply, for example, political or religious ideology or symbolize national traditions or geographical features. For example, the flag of Venezuela features three vertical stripes of yellow, blue, and red, which represent the (yellow) wealth of the New World, eventually separated from Spain after a long bloody (red) battle by the (blue) ocean in between.

Of course, it can also, as in many European flags, display livery colors, which are heraldic shades that do not convey any symbolic meaning. The seven heraldic shades that remain popular in flag design are the metals gold and silver, which are represented on flags by yellow and white, and the five colors red, blue, green, black, and purple.

As in the Venezuelan flag, red symbolizes the bloodshed of patriots, but—since time immemorial—it has also signaled danger and come to represent revolution and socialism. Green represents safety, vegetation, youth, hope, and Islam; white is used to convey peace, surrender, and truce; orange is for courage and sacrifice; yellow is for sickness and caution; and black is for mourning, death and anarchy. Certain color combinations are also symbolic. The colors of the French tricolor are a symbol of liberty, while white and pale blue represent peace, which is why the United Nations uses them. As a general rule of thumb, the optimum number of colors that should be used in a flag is three and light colors should be placed next to darker ones.

The colors of sea flags generally follow the colors of those on land. Probably the only exception is the pirate flag, which is usually black (representing "no mercy will be shown to those who resist") and carries symbols of death, such as the skull and crossbones, with the aim of terrifying victims.

Flag Proportions & Sizes

The proportions of a flag, in other words the ratio of the width to the length, are also important, as although all rectangular flags look like they should be made in the ratio 1:2, that is not necessarily their official size. For example, the official proportions for the US flag are 10:19. For the sake of uniformity, however, organizers of international events do usually adopt the same proportions for flags that are displayed together, which can lead to the distortion of some of the flags' design elements.

The width of a flag is measured along the hoist, while the length is measured from the hoist to the fly end of a rectangular flag, and from the hoist to the apex of a triangle in triangular and swallow-tailed flags. In the navy, however, flags are measured in breadths along the width, rather than the yards or meters along the length of a flag maker. Thus, a flag measuring 1.8 meters by 3.7 meters is called a flag of eight breadths in the navy, while a flag maker will refer to it as a flag of four yards. A breadth represents 23 centimeters, equivalent to the width of traditional bunting.

Generally speaking, flags used to be larger in the days of old. For example, rectangular flags in the British navy in the 17th century measured around eight meters by 16 meters at their largest. They remained this size throughout the 18th century, but in the 19th century started being made slightly smaller, around six meters by 12 meters, and under Queen Victoria they were smaller still.

In the 17th century, signal flags were the same size as the regular command flags and ensigns hoisted on particular parts of the ship. However, when numerary flag codes were introduced at the end of the 18th century, which meant that three or four signal flags had to be hoisted on a single masthead, they became smaller. The most common sizes for signal flags of the International Code today are a) two meters by 2.4 meters; b) 1.4 meters by 1.7 meters; and c) 0.8 meters by 0.9 meters.

Since the reign of Queen Victoria, the proportions of naval sea flags have also been standardized, so that ensigns and jacks are made in a ratio of 1:2, while the admirals' flags are in a proportion of 2:3. Merchant shipping house flags are not covered by official dictates, but are most commonly made in a proportion of 2:3.

Flag Materials

The earliest modern flags were made from wool or—if destined for use by sovereigns or their envoys—silk taffeta or silk damask. From the early Middle Ages, the silk was decorated with colorful designs created using appliqué, gold leaf, chain stitch or flat stitch, or a combination of all these techniques. Later, between the 14th and 16th centuries, the ornamentation became even more elaborate, featuring emblems of painted leather, silver or gold cord trimmings, small gold spangles, delicate embroidery and pearls. This trend for painted and/or embroidered flags continued right up until the 19th century. The finest examples of this kind of flag are the so-called Julius banners, which are the war flags that Pope Julius II presented to the Swiss in 1512 as a token of his appreciation for supplying the Protectors of the Liberty of the Church—the Swiss Guards who still protect the Vatican to this day. It was the more general purpose flags, used by the army on land and by merchant or war vessels at sea, that were made of wool and other, cheaper, fabrics, such as linen and bunting (a coarse, loosely woven material). The emblems on these flags tended to be painted, rather than embroidered.

Since the 20th century, flags have been made from bright synthetic fabrics designed to fulfil the numerous requirements of outdoor flags. The ideal fabrics are either heavyweight, two-ply polyester or a fabric that is 25 per cent wool and 75 per cent nylon. These fabrics not only make the flag look lustrous, they also have superb wearing strength, and are washable, fire-resistant, mildew-resistant, and mothproof. In addition, they are light, which enables the flag to fly well—even in the rain.

As far as sea flags are concerned, we know that the flags on the fleet of Henry VIII (1491–1547) were very ornate, being made with gold and silver leaf, gold and silver thread, and silk fringes. Flags for ordinary everyday use, however, were made of cheaper linen or woollen cloth, and the flag of St. George was made from red and white material, rather than painted. When Queen Elizabeth I sent her fleet against the Spanish Armada in the 16th century, she spent heavily on lavish flags, but the elaborate heraldic banners and streamers of the Tudor era soon gave way to more hard-wearing woollen flags. During the 18th and 19th centuries, 100 per cent wool bunting was the favored material for British naval flags. It was only in 1955 that the navy abandoned the all-wool formula for 75 per cent nylon, 25 per cent wool worsted. Even more recently, 100 per cent synthetic materials—first nylon, now polyester—have been adopted.

Flag Manufacture

In the past, the production of flags was a very labor intensive process. Today, due to greater usage, the costs involved and, also, the fact that designs are so much simpler, most flags are mass produced in factories, although a few special ones are still individually made by hand.

The production of a flag usually follows a path similar to the one described here. The art department of the flag factory prepares and stores the paper patterns of flag designs, which are sent to the cutting department so that it can provide the sewing department with pieces of fabric in the exact sizes and colors needed. The factory will have dyed large pieces of fabric with chemical dyes that penetrate material fibres so well it is almost impossible to tell which side of the fabric is the reverse. When the sewing department comes to assemble the flags, the correctly colored pieces of fabric are joined together by double seams using color-matched thread. The top and bottom hems are made with two rows of stitching, while the hem at the fly-end has four rows of lock stitching with backstitch reinforcement. Finally, the hoist is usually inserted and sewn into a heavy white canvas heading (through which a rope can be threaded to enable the flag to be attached to a flagpole), either with eyelets or with the rope sewn in. In Japan, triangular pieces of canvas are used to reinforce the hoist corners.

Once the pieces of fabric have been stitched together, any emblems that might feature on the flag are appliquéd or embroidered (using computer-aided machinery) on to the base material. Simple emblems, such as stars, fleurs-de-lis, crescents and crosses are pasted on, while large emblems are pasted on and then reinforced with stitching around the edges. In the finishing department, the heading and grommets are added to outdoor flags, and indoor and parade flags are fitted with tabs and fringes.

Flag Accessories & Hardware

Once the flags are made, they are ready to be flown, which requires a few extra accessories and hardware. Flags may be flown from a flag pole or the halyard of a sailing ship, carried on a staff or spear, fixed on a pin to stand on a table, or hung from a spar at a 45 degree angle to the vertical.

Flags for flying from a flagpole have a hollow tube or heading on the hoist side. Those made in Europe usually have a hoist rope sewn into the sleeve that can be attached to the *halyard* (the rope used to hoist and lower the flag) with a *becket* and *toggle* (the toggle is at the top end of the hoist rope, the becket is at the top end of the halyard). In America, the flag's heading has an eyelet at either end to which clips on the halyard are attached. In Japan, the hoist edges are reinforced with triangles of heavy canvas, through which ribbons are fed and then attached to the clips on the halyard.

Flagpoles make it possible to fly a flag at a certain height. A flagpole consists of a pole made of glass fiber, aluminium, steel, or wood, with a *truck* (containing a pulley) on the top. Above the truck is a cap, either in the simple form of a disc or in the more decorative form of a ball or eagle. The bottom part of the flag pole is usually embedded in solid concrete foundations, or permanently welded to a base made of heavy cast aluminium. The halyard passes through the truck's pulley and is secured to a *cleat* (a device with two prongs that project horizontally in opposite directions from a central base) on the lower part of the flagpole.

The flag of Mexico waves in front of the Palacio Nacional.

For indoor or parade use, when greater rigidity is required in the flag, a range of devices are used to attach the flag to the staff. In Europe, the most popular device is to fasten the heading of the flag to the staff with special decorative nails. Traditionally, these nails carry engraved emblems, along with the names of the institutions or individuals that founded the flag or color. In the United States, the heading has leather tabs at each end, which attach to screwheads protruding from the staff. In Japan, instead of a heading, there are two or three leather triangles with eyelets that enable the flag to be fastened to the staff with decorative tasseled cords. Indoor flags often also feature a fringe, a decorative tasseled cord and the ribbons of an order, which are often attached to the decorative finial at the end of the staff. To make heavy parade flags easier to carry, the flag bearers wear flag belts—an idea that probably developed from the time of Japanese

Samurai warriors, who carried their flags strapped to their backs so that they had both hands free for fighting.

In the 16th century, heraldic banners and ensigns at sea were usually fastened to their flagstaffs or provided with sockets that slipped over the staffs, so that they could be carried ashore if necessary. These days, the most common method of attaching the flag to the halyard is by the becket and toggle method, although the Royal Navy tends to use Inglefield clips, interlocking metal swivel slips that engage with others on the hoist and halyard and have a quick release mechanism.

Flag Etiquette

Some countries have very strict codes detailing the way in which their national flag should be treated. The United States is one and has laid down a whole set of rules on flag etiquette. For example, the Stars and Stripes has to be folded up in a certain way: twice lengthways and then folded into triangular sections until it is reduced to a small bundle that can be easily stored. Britain, however, is at the opposite end of the spectrum and has no rules regarding the Union Jack, hence its usage on all manner of objects from underwear to novelty items and high fashion.

Having said that, enough countries have adopted rules for their flags, which have so much in common that it is possible to formulate general guidelines for international flag usage. For example, most countries follow a set of rules for the raising of their national flag at home. While it is being hoisted a person indicates respect by facing the flag, standing to attention, and remaining silent until the flag has been fully raised. In fact, it is possible for a flag to be saluted at any time, and—in doing so—that person is honoring the country, principles, or person that the flag represents, but it is most often saluted when hoisted, passed in a parade review or the national anthem is played. The flag is supposed to be displayed from sunrise to sunset, except on days when there is bad weather. And if it is displayed at night, it must be well illuminated. When it is finally lowered, it should be done in a dignified, ceremonious manner.

Because the national flag takes precedence over all other flags, it is also important that it is not displayed in a position inferior to any other flag. When the national flags of several countries are flown together—for example, at the headquarters of international organizations, at international conferences, and at major sporting events—then they should all be displayed at the same height on separate flagpoles of the same size. Despite their official proportions, they should also be of the same size (or at least the same width). Traditionally, they are also flown in alphabetical order, either in the official language of the host country or in English. When the flagpoles form an enclosed circle, as they often do outside an international building, the alphabetical order of the flags should be clockwise, with the first flag positioned opposite the main entrance.

There are also guidelines for the displaying of national flags with other flags that do not belong to other countries. Examples of these kinds of flags include those linked to a region or province, a county, parish or commune, a civic body, the services, and a university, school, or corporation. When one of these flags is displayed with the national flag, the national flag should be on the left of the observer. In a line of three flags, the national flag should be positioned in the center, while in a line of four, the national flag should be the first to appear on the observer's left. If there's a line of five or more flags, two national flags should be used—one at either end of the line. In a

The flags of different nations are given equal precedence at international events.

semi-circle, the national flag should be in the center, while in an enclosed circle, the national flag should be positioned in the center, immediately opposite the main entrance to the building or arena.

Although flags—particularly those with coats of arms or emblems—are designed to be flown in a horizontal position, there are occasions (on a table, against a wall and down the middle of a street) when they may be displayed vertically. In these circumstances, the general rule to be observed is that the upper edge of the national flag should be to the observer's left (so that the observer sees the reverse of the flag). In addition, when a flag is displayed vertically in the middle of a street, its top edge should be to the north in an east-west street and to the east in a north-south street. However, do not immediately assume that all national flags can be hung in this manner. Some countries, such as Brazil, Pakistan, Saudi Arabia, and Sri Lanka, explicitly forbid the vertical display of their national flags, while others, like Liechtenstein, Slovakia, and Slovenia, have

actually produced special designs for displaying their national flags in a vertical position, and Germany and Austria turn their coats of arms upright in state flags that hang vertically.

Other rules governing the general use of flags include the following. When a national flag is carried in a procession, it should always be held aloft and free—as at the Olympic Games opening ceremony, when one athlete is chosen to hold the national flag at the

Flags used in processions should be carried in a dignified manner and never be allowed to drag on the ground.

head of the team as it walks around the stadium. When a flag is displayed from a staff on a speaker's platform, it should be on the speaker's right as he faces the audience. The national flag should always be used in a dignified manner, so it should never be used as a table or seat cover, or as drapery of any sort, and it should never be used as a receptacle for receiving, holding, carrying or delivering anything. In the same manner, it should never touch the ground, the floor, or water, except at funerals, when a flag dragging on the ground is employed as a mark of respect.

Interestingly, death and flags have been inextricably linked since the 16th century, when it became customary for ships to half-mast their flags to indicate a death or mourning. The origin of this ancient custom has never been ascertained, but it was subsequently transferred to land so that now flags on flagpoles are half-masted. Flags can also be used to cover a coffin—as at the funeral of Diana, Princess of Wales, when a Royal Standard was used—when the hoist is placed at the head and the top edge is over the left shoulder.

Even flags flown on ships have their own set of etiquette, which has developed over time. For example, when a ship is in harbor, it must hoist the ensign at eight o'clock in the morning local time and lower it again at sunset. And, when merchant ships pass, they salute one another by dipping their flags.

While many of these rules may seem petty, it is very important that they are followed because they are a crucial part of diplomatic protocol and, if not always observed correctly, the results can be disastrous. For example, there was an occasion when an Iranian delegation to a European country almost abandoned talks because the hosts placed the flag of Iran used by the overthrown Shah regime on their table, rather than the modern version. And the incorrect vertical display of some flags can cause serious consternation, because—for example—it means the Polish flag becomes the flag of Monaco or Indonesia and the Dutch flag becomes that of Yugoslavia.

THE HISTORY OF FLAGS

Symbolism and Standards: Precursors to the Modern Flag

Anthropological studies have revealed that totemism (the belief in kinship of groups or individuals having a common totem or symbol) has always played an integral part in the life of man. Even in the very early days of civilization, hunting and food gathering people lived in small nomadic groups. Several groups would consider themselves related by bands of kinship, with the larger social unit thought of as a clan or tribe. Each clan adopted an animal, plant, or other natural phenomenon as its totem, representations of which became a symbol of the clan's unity. And, eventually, the clan came to assume the name of its totem.

The representations, which were usually carved out of wood or stone, had similar functions to the flags of today: they showed loyalty and were a method of sending signals. Each clan elected a leader for the purpose of making collective decisions and, to distinguish him from his peers, he would use a long decorated staff (at the top of which a carved totem was placed), as well as ceremonial clothes and a headdress. The staff—technically known as a vexilloid—was used to rally the clan when it went to war and to point out the direction of a march or attack. (Think of how a guide leads a tour group through a crowded street using a flag these days and you will have some idea of how the staff was used.)

Totemism took place in every corner of the globe, without the individual groups knowing that it was happening elsewhere. Perhaps this is not surprising, given that socio-psychological experiments have shown that groups with a strong feeling of common interest and solidarity tend to inject their community spirit into something concrete. Thus the totem came to represent the unity of the group and readily acquired a certain halo of sanctity—it's a sentiment that is reflected in the logos and corporate identities of most large corporations in the modern era.

Many years ago, in what is now America, bands or tribes of the Dakota people (who inhabited the Mississippi and Missouri river basins) named themselves after animals, such as the snake, tortoise, wolf, and buffalo, and used a symbol of their animal to distinguish themselves from other groups. Many believed that

A Haida tribe totem pole depicting a bird stands in Canada.

their ancestors had evolved from the animals or inanimate objects that had become their symbol. Similarly, the Tswana tribes of southern Africa are named after certain animals, indicating that they too held animals in high regard and probably worshipped them: the Bakwena are "the crocodile people," while the Bakgatla are "the monkey people."

A large number of Indian tribes, for example the Santhals, were (and still are) organized on a totemic basis—and they worship mostly plants and animals as well. In many ways, they regard the totem as a guardian angel. For while it demands great respect, with the bodies of clan members being painted with representations of their animal or plant on solemn occasions, it is also expected to look after the clan. Sacred, traditional, and a rallying point for the community, it served as a symbol of hope and victory for those who worshipped it in the unceasing struggle for survival during ancient times. The need to better display their sacred motif on the battlefield led the Santhals to create a wooden vexilloid known as "dhvaja." Carried into war, it inspired combatants to victory. It was also used to mark out the lines and stations of encampment, and to keep different bands in order when marching into battle.

Roman vexilloids carried various animals, each with their own significance.

However, the oldest known vexilloid still in existence is to be found on a piece of Egyptian pottery of the Gerzean period (3400 BC). These vexilloids, which were usually made from wood, were painted with representations of gods, "nomes" (the provinces of pre-dynastic Egypt), or both, as a number of the nomes were named after local gods. However, much like the other clans around the world, some of the totems were also crafted from the natural world and featured birds such as falcons and ibises, which were depicted as highly stylized emblems on the vexilloids. These staffs appear to have been used as signs for soldiers to follow and, upon defeat or dispersion of the troops, to return to regroup. The oldest vexilloid still in existence is only a little younger, dating to around 5,000 years ago. It consists of a metal pole, with a finial in the form of an eagle and a square metal "flag" covered with reliefs.

It is another few thousand years, around 1500 BC, before we have solid evidence that vexilloids were also being used in China. At that time, we know that the Chinese used a bamboo staff topped with a metal trident, from which hung small rings with tassels made of horses' tails. Some staffs also bore figures from myth and nature, such as dragons, tigers, sparrows, snakes, and tortoises. The number of narrow ribbons attached to the outer edge of the staff denoted the social rank of the flag-bearer—if there were 12, it belonged to the Emperor, but if there was only one, it was the mark of a low ranking official. To turn

Each Roman unit carried its own "signum"—a lance with a silver plated shaft.

it into a signal for battle, a long, wide, swallow-tailed ribbon was attached to the vexilloid.

Much later, in the ninth and eighth centuries BC, the Assyrians (the early inhabitants of present day Iraq) also used vexilloids. They expanded their empire through a series of military campaigns, during which they carried their vexilloids—many of which bore pictures of an archer on a bull's back or of two bulls—on foot or attached to their war chariots.

The Romans started using staffs after Hannibal, the Carthagenian, attacked the Roman Empire in 217 BC carrying vexilloids, and they really made it their own. Each unit of the Roman army had its own staff (known as a "signum"), which consisted of a lance with a silver-plated shaft, topped with a crosspiece carrying figures of various beasts, the most famous (and most important) of which featured an eagle ("aquila"). According to Pliny the Elder, "Gaius Marius in his second consulship (103 BC) assigned the eagle exclusively to the Roman legions. Before that period, it had only held the first rank, there being four others as well—the wolf, the minotaur, the horse, and the wild boar—each of which preceded a single division." Below the shaft hung several metal rings forming a laurel wreath, to which were attached medallions with portraits of the emperor and members of the imperial house.

It is interesting to note that vexilloids remained popular at this time and much later, even though the modern flag had already appeared. For example, in the 13th century, the Mongols carried an instantly recognizable vexilloid that consisted of a staff topped with a metal ball or spear, with a horse's tail attached to it—signifying Genghis Khan's many conquests on horseback. Later, vexilloids became the sign of a commander in the Turkish Army and, in the 17th and 18th centuries, they were carried before the commanders-in-chief of the Polish Army. Even today, English drum majors, the leaders of military bands, carry a "baton," which could be considered akin to a vexilloid.

The Making of the Modern Flag

The first modern flag was probably no more than a piece of cloth tied to a stick, but it was used in much the same way as we use flags today: to attract attention or send a message. We know, for example, that a red flag has always indicated danger. But where was the first flag created? China and India are considered the two most likely candidates, with the former being the stronger contender because the Chinese were the first to make cloth out of silk. This strong, lightweight fabric made an excellent flag. Being lighter and much more easily visible from a greater distance than a vexilloid, it was much more practical. One of the first flag references dates to 1122 BC, when the founding Emperor of the Chou dynasty in China had a white flag carried before him to announce his presence.

The first mention of a European flag is made by Greek writers, who referred to a purple flag being the sign of the admiral's ship in the Athenian navy at the end

Carried by a Roman officer of Augustus' 2nd Legion, this vexillum is typically Roman.

of the fifth century BC. But the first flag we know to have existed in the West appears in a huge mosaic from Pompeii (that has since been moved in the National Museum in Naples), which shows Alexander the Great defeating the Persians in around 330 BC. It features a staff with an almost square piece of cloth, the bottom edge of which is fringed, hanging from a crossbar. Although now eroded, the red field of the square cloth bore an image of a golden cock, according to sketches made when the mosaic was discovered in 1831. To be absolutely precise, this type of flag—because it flies from the horizontal—is known as a banner.

Around 200 years later, a flag of exactly the same shape and mounted on a staff in the same way was adopted by the Roman cavalry and named "vexillum"— from which the term vexillology was developed. The Romans used the vexillum as a tactical distinguishing mark to enable one detachment of a legion to be recognized by another. The cloth of the vexillum was either red or purple and was sometimes decorated with the name of the cavalry unit or an emblem or a portrait of the emperor. The cloth was fastened by its upper edge or two top corners from the crossbar so that it always looked draped and there was often a heavy fringe on the bottom edge.

Another flag that was popular in the Roman Army from the second century AD was the "draco" (or dragon flag), borrowed from the Parthians or Sarmatians (the inhabitants of present-day India and the Ukraine, respectively) who had used this kind of flag several centuries earlier. The draco comprised a staff, at the top of which sat a hollow bronze dragon's head with a long, skinny silk windsock attached. When the wind blew, the windsock zigzagged like a serpent and a device in the dragon's head made a whistling noise. The dragon flag was also used in Britain during the Dark Ages and, in the sixth century, was adopted by the Saxon conquerors. Both the Anglo-Saxon and Norman armies used it until at least the 12th century. And it is to them that we owe the word flag, because it is generally accepted that it is derived from an old Saxon or Germanic word "fflaken" or "ffleogan," meaning to fly or flap in the wind. A flag, therefore, is something that is free to be agitated by the wind.

It was around the sixth century that the Byzantine army started using a square or rectangular flag (with one or two triangular tongues extending from the top edge) that was flown horizontally, rather than the Roman "vexillum" or banner. Over the next 200 years, use of this type of flag, which—without the tongues—was very similar in shape to most present-day national flags, spread throughout Central Europe. It was probably from this flag that the gonfanon developed at the very beginning of the ninth century.

The first evidence of a gonfanon was found in a mosaic commemorating the crowning of Charlemagne as Emperor that Pope Leo III (circa 750–816 AD) had placed in the Triclinium of the Lateran Palace in Rome in about 800 AD. According to contemporary sources (as the original mosaic has not survived), Christ was handing the keys of the church to Pope Sylvester and a flag to Constantine on the right-hand side of the picture, while St. Peter presented a cloak to Pope Leo and a flag to Charlemagne on the left-hand side. It is said that the green field of the gonfanon handed to Charlemagne was sprinkled with gold and bore six concentric rings of red, black, and gold. This event led to the ceremonial presentation of flags by ecclesiastical authorities to rulers or leaders of expeditions approved by the Church becoming commonplace. Emperors, too, started handing out flags to their favored subjects.

A little earlier, in the 8th century, the Arabs had begun to utilize triangular flags that were plain black or white, although they later increased the range of colors they used and added religious inscriptions and geometric ornaments—a religious ban prevented them from employing representational art. However, the most famous triangular flag emerged toward the end of the ninth century. The Vikings' celebrated Raven Flag, about which there are many stories of magical properties and mystery, is said to have been the first flag to fly in North America. Although there are no illustrations or accurate descriptions of the flag, Northumbrian coins dating to that era feature a heavily fringed triangular flag flown vertically with the upper edge horizontal.

Similar flags can be seen in the Bayeux Tapestry, made from 1067 to 1077, which contains more than 70 embroidered scenes of William, Duke of Normandy's invasion of England in 1066. A flag virtually identical to the Vikings'

Raven is carried immediately behind William the Conqueror. By this time, flags were obviously well established and there is a proliferation of gonfanons in the tapestry, as well as a large number of Norman flags bearing a cross, which was then the main emblem used by both the military and maritime forces. Interestingly, the tapestry also features the dragon standard of the English King Harold, which begs the question: how did the dragon come to be such a prominent symbol in the west as well as the Orient?

William (carrying the flag) is approached by a man bringing him his horse, in the Bayeux Tapestry.

The dragon, alongside the tiger, hawk, turtle, and snake, was certainly one of the most common flag symbols used in China. And when flag usage spread to nearby countries such as Burma, Siam, and other parts of South East Asia, gold embroidered elephants and bulls were used on white, yellow, or black backgrounds. Perhaps it's because all these animals could be considered predators in their own environment that they were so popular during times of great unrest and conflict.

And, just as in the West, Chinese flags changed from being square to triangular with "flammules" (flame-shaped edges). It was a move echoed by the Mongols, when—led by the great Kublai Khan—they conquered China in 1279 and began to use triangular flags with flammules, which were mounted sideways on staffs topped with the Chinese trident. Eventually, flammules were also added to the trident and horses' tails were attached to its base.

But no matter how the flags' shapes changed over time, the hierarchy of Chinese society was always reflected in the large number of different types of flag used by the emperor, nobility, commanders of the imperial army, and governors of the provinces and counties. For example, in the 19th century, there were nine different levels of mandarin (as a member of the bureaucracy was known in the Chinese empire) and the army used some 50 different flags; there were also special flags for 11 ranks of envoys.

So, all over the world, the earliest flags were rallying points used by leaders to spur their communities to war and, for that reason, often featured fierce animals, such as tigers and dragons, that were considered a symbol of strength. To this day, many flags still bear these figures. (For example, the British standard

has a lion and the state flag of Wyoming carries a bison.) Carried into battle either by hand or attached to elephants or chariots (whichever method of transport the warring factions used), it was always the first object of attack in battle, because its fall meant confusion and, ultimately, defeat. And, if an invading army was successful, the first thing it did was plant its own flag on the walls of the captured city, thereby laying claim to its new territory, such was the importance

The flag of Wales, featuring the totemic dragon.

attached to a flag. In fact, great respect was commanded by flags, because—effectively—they were royal flags, being associated with the "king" or tribal chief. Sometimes to touch the flag bearer was even a punishable crime.

Heraldry: Further Flag Development

From the seventh century, however, heraldry (literally, the art of producing and recording individuals' coats of arms) started to gain a foothold. This need for each knight to have his own coat of arms, which was usually displayed on his shield, became increasingly important as full body armor and the use of a helmet to cover and protect his face became ever more popular. If, in battle, a knight came across another knight dressed in full chain mail armor and a helmet, how was he to tell whether he was an ally or enemy, unless he was displaying a coat of arms?

Of course, another reason coats of arms became necessary was due to the widespread use of the cross by all the armed forces in Western Europe. Religious symbols were among the first to be expressed in flag form: Christian armies carried the Cross into battle and

Use of identifying motifs became increasingly important as armor covered the combatants faces and bodies.

the Virgin Mary was depicted on the banners of several Roman Catholic countries. By the time of the Norman invasion of England, a large number of flags with crosses were in use and, some 30 years later, at the time of the First Crusade, even more banners with the sign of the cross had appeared. According to the "Gesta Regis Henrici Secundi" by Benedict Abbas, which is the oldest known account of flags with crosses, on January 13, 1188, the Kings of England and France (and their men) received a white and red cross respectively, while the Count of Flanders (and his men) received a green cross. Similarities among crosses such as these could cause major misunderstandings in the heat of the moment on the battlefield, but an individual coat of arms left no doubt as to the identification of a knight.

The flag of Tunisia featuring the crescent moon that is the official emblem of Islam.

It was probably the Muslim Arabs, known during the Crusades as the Saracens, who introduced the idea of heraldic arms to Europe. From about 630 AD, they started conquering vast tracts of land around the Mediterranean. Forbidden by Islamic principles from carrying the depiction of God or people on their flags that could have been seen as idolatrous, their flags were very simple. With a background of plain black, white, red, or green, they bore a crescent moon—an Assyrian sacred symbol dating to at least the ninth century BC, if not before—that has become the official symbol of Islam, although a crescent and star combination and a double-bladed sword representing the Prophet's son-in-law Ali are also used to symbolize Islam today.

Black was chosen because it was considered the color of vengeance (and was supposed to have been the color of Mohammed's banner). Green was the color picked by the Fatimid dynasty (908–1171), who claimed to be descendants of Fatima, the youngest daughter of Mohammed, and it later became the color most closely associated with Islam. But, most importantly for reasons of heraldry, flags carried by individuals also had an inscription that helped to identify the bearer as a particular person.

The basic rules of heraldry were adopted after the Second Crusade (1147–49), when returning knights took the idea of customized arms back home with them. The term heraldry developed because it was heralds who organized jousting tournaments, which were very popular at the time, and controlled what contestants put on their shields to distinguish themselves. These tournaments provided the perfect opportunity for knights from all over Europe to meet and exhibit their proficiency in handling a horse and weapons, and for heralds to present personal shields to participants.

Many pre-heraldic devices were incorporated into coats of arms, including the Christian cross, the lion, eagle, griffin, horse, fleur-de-lis, rose, and various weapons, but never before had so many been placed together on a single flag—and with an emphasis, of course, on symbols that were relevant to the history or background of the bearer's family. A knight's shield provided the ideal background for these emblems. In portraying the various devices, the arms bearer was limited to seven heraldic tinctures—five colors (red, blue, green, black, and purple) and two metals (gold and silver)—and to achieve the best possible identification from a distance, the rule of alternation was adopted, which forbade putting color on color or metal on metal. A "fimbriation," or border, of metal was used to separate adjacent areas of two colors. In addition to the shield, a coat of arms consisted of supporters on either side of the shield, a helmet with a wreath, mantling, and a crest on top of the shield—a scroll and a motto appear to have been optional extras. Although, initially, arms were granted to one person only, and were not to be used by anyone else, it soon became customary to pass a coat of arms from father to son, and they therefore became closely linked with genealogy.

The invention of heraldry also led to a rapid growth in personal flags, because everybody entitled to a coat of arms was also qualified to carry an armorial banner—and it is interesting to note that the design devices used on the personal heraldic badges of rulers did not necessarily relate to their coats of arms. Some of the most famous heraldic design devices on badges include the white and red

A design featuring the red rose of Lancaster from 15th century England.

roses of York and Lancaster from the 15th century War of the Roses, the white boar of Richard III, the porcupine of Louis XII, and the radiant sun of Louis XIV.

The principal kind of flag was an armorial banner that was either square or much wider than it was long, the sizes of which varied according to the rank of its owner, with the largest flag belonging to the person of greatest importance, in other words, the emperor. According to one medieval source, the banner of an emperor was 1.8 meters square, while that of a king was 1.5 meters square, that of a prince 1.2 meters square and that of an earl, marquis, viscount, or baron, 0.9 meters square.

Another important armorial flag was the standard, which—during the time of Edward III of England in around 1350—came to describe the banner of an influential noble, or member of a royal house. Why the word "standard" was chosen to describe the flag is obscure, because, originally, a standard was an emblem that "stood by itself," but its use is not: it was designed to indicate the rallying point or headquarters of the arms-bearer, or "armiger." Not unlike a pennant, it was a long, tapering flag, with a rounded swallow-tail, which bore the livery colors arranged horizontally. The hoist carried either the national mark (such as the English cross of St. George) or a coat of arms in the form of an armorial banner. Next appeared the heraldic badge of the arms-bearer with his motto, and then another badge or crest, and around the edge was either a border of pieces in the livery color or a rich fringe. Heraldic standards and ensigns such as these are still used at Highland gatherings in Scotland, where the standard of the chief is set up outside his tent and is used to rally his clansmen.

Only the arms-bearer could carry his banner or standard, so three other types of flag, which also carried his personal heraldic design devices, were used by his esquires: the guidon, pennon, and badge-flag. The guidon was a simpler version of the standard. It was also tapered but was shorter, and bore the national device on the inner edge and a badge on the livery colors. It was used on horseback, and was a precursor to the archers' guidon. The pennon was a swallow-tailed flag carried on a mounted warrior's lance. In most cases, it bore the badge on a background in the livery colors. The badge-flag was a rectangular flag with the background divided in the livery colors, bearing the heraldic badge or badges.

It is interesting to note that from the early stages of heraldry, coats of arms were also adopted and used by ecclesiastics and military orders, such as the Knights Templar, the Knights of St. John of Jerusalem, great Spanish and Portuguese orders, and the Teutonic Knights. However, the arms and armorial banners embraced by bishops and the abbots of monasteries were not regarded as personifying the individuals, but the orders that they represented; they were also signs of their domains. Jumping on the bandwagon, guilds and universities began to obtain charters from the

The coat of arms of the Washington family.

crown and were granted arms as well. The guild flags often bore the most obvious of devices—a black flag with three white candles, for example, represented the candlemakers of Bayeux in France. Then, it was the turn of the towns to gain arms and, finally, there were civic armorial banners, which became the real national flags for the burghers because they symbolized their rights and privileges.

Picture all these flags in usage on a battlefield and you can imagine what an imposing scene it must have been. There were royal banners and banners of knights and all their esquires, plus all the flags of the ecclesiastics, provinces, cities, and guilds. For example, when the French and English armies met at Buironfosse in 1339, the French forces displayed a total of 220 banners and 560 pennons. And, at the battle of Tannenberg in 1410, the 56 banners unfurled by the Teutonic knights and the 91 banners by the Polish Lithuanian forces were mainly the emblems of cities and provinces.

A 14th century battle scene.

In the Middle Ages, banners were not, however, only used during times of fighting. When not carried into battle, the largest and most elaborate were usually to be found proudly displayed on city walls, castle towers and civic buildings, or being carried triumphantly in marches and processions marking saints' days and important local festivals. There was a very strong association between flags and the church, too. Every single flag carried into battle was consecrated in the church and, if not on display around the town, was kept there in peacetime. And just as for humans, the church became the final resting place of all flags when they had passed their sell-by date and no longer served a purpose. As a result of this association, most of the banners used on the battlefield in the Middle Ages served to identify states, provinces, cities, and guilds at a later stage. In fact, to this day many cities in Central Europe and Italy use the same flags as in medieval times.

Of course, some of the flags used at this time were not armorial—they were purely allied with the church and made extensive use of Christian symbols, such as the representation of the Holy Trinity, the Virgin Mary, the Holy Ghost and the Crucifixion, in non-heraldic form. Then there were banners with symbols of the saints, such as the cross of St. George or the lion of St. Mark, and banners that displayed the actual figures of saints with their attributes, the most popular of which were St. Peter with his keys, St. Andrew with a diagonal cross, a mounted St. George slaying the dragon, and St. Catherine with her wheel. These flags were popular across Europe, with the lion of St. Mark being the emblem of the Republic of Venice, St. Peter's keys the emblem of the papacy and St. Andrew's cross the national symbol of Scotland (in a slightly different form, it also came to be associated with Burgundy and Spain at a later stage).

At the end of the 16th century, when European countries began to build professional armies based on permanent groupings of troops in legions and regiments, banners began to lose their heraldic character. The French really set an example in 1597, when they developed consistent designs for individual regiments and companies. These "Colors" (as military flags are called) often consisted of two sets of flags: those that were elaborately decorated with embroidered coats of arms and more durable, much simpler flags for use in battle. The latter served their purpose on the battlefield until the end of the 19th century, when modern warfare made the function of colors in battle pretty much obsolete. (There are, though, several instances of troops displaying their colors as late as in the Second World War.) Today, the more fancy military Colors are still used, but only for ceremonial purposes.

A man dressed in samurai battle armor among symbolically decorated flags for the Hojo Godai Festival.

Although we think of heraldry as principally a European thing, in the tenth century the Japanese developed a similar use of symbols, known as "mon," quite independently of what was happening in the western world. These "mons" are the equivalent of the heraldic badge rather than the heraldic figure. The only difference between the two heraldic systems is that mons do not appear on a shield; in all other respects they play the same role as in Europe.

The symbols on Japanese badges are usually symmetrical, simple, and highly stylized representations of flowers (mallow, apricot, wisteria), birds (crane, wild goose) and everyday objects (fan, arrow, hatchet) or, alternatively, typically Japanese geometric designs. The Emperor's standard, for example, is a stylized chrysanthemum that does not really resemble the real thing. Unlike European devices, there are no specific heraldic colors.

Like arms, the mons were traditionally used on banners, armor, and the clothes of the retainers of great lords, as well as to decorate castles, carriages, lanterns, and the belongings of the individual and his family. Interestingly, the heraldic banners used in Japan in the Middle Ages differ from the European ones in that their width was several times greater than their length; this provided plenty of room for the mon to be repeated several times. Both these banners, and the much smaller Japanese "sashimono" banners, were fastened into a socket attached to the back of a piece of armor covering the chest and back known as a cuirass—this meant that the Samurai warriors had both hands free for fighting.

Today, mons are still widely used, and are just as likely to appear as decoration on fans and clothing as they are on modern banners, which are rectangular and display the mon right in their center. As hereditary symbols, it has been a legal requirement that they must be registered ever since the 17th century. And, just as in Europe, the mons, which have always been passed down through families, have more recently been adopted by cities and regions.

The First National Flags

So far, we've seen first vexilloids and then flags used for military and ceremonial purposes, but by the 12th century they had also started to identify rulers and their domains, as well as nationality at sea. The first piece of evidence that exists to confirm this fact is a manuscript, attributed to a Spanish Franciscan friar, that depicts the flags of North Africa and the Middle East. Written and illuminated in about 1350, it has a long rambling title, which translates into English roughly as the "Book of the Knowledge of All the Kingdoms, Countries, and Lordships that there are in the World, and of the Ensigns and Arms of Each Country and Lordship; also of the Kings and Lords Who Govern Them." Even though some of the friar's accounts are not entirely reliable, the text is of value because it is the earliest account of flags of all nations, some 100 of which are illustrated.

Certainly, even of those flags that the friar did depict correctly, not many are still used as national flags today. This is partly because many of the original flags represented an individual, such as a sovereign, and countries tended to abandon personal flags in favor of a design that had some national significance, which often meant that they were religious. Many adopted the flag of their patron saint, like England which adopted the cross of St. George in the 13th century. The personal flags were not abandoned altogether, however, as they often became the king's standard, flown only when he was present. Of course, another reason why the original flags no longer exist is because boundaries have changed. It does mean, however, that some states, provinces, counties, and cities have flags of great historical interest because they represent an ancient kingdom/principality that has now been incorporated into a nation.

The first modern style flag was the Dutch revolutionary "Prinsenvlag," which consisted of three horizontal stripes (colored orange, white, and blue) of equal size and was adapted from the flags under which the Netherlands fought for independence from Spain in the 16th century. Orange was chosen to represent their leader, William of Orange, while blue and white were used as they were Christian colors. This flag marked a change in the design of flags: instead of complicated heraldic devices, plain stripes were being used. When the United States and France both gained independence in the late 18th century, they followed suit by creating the simple flags that remain their national flags up until the present day.

Through their design, these newly created flags aimed to convey the feeling that the monarchy had been abolished and, with it, the heraldic system of identification had also been rejected. Instead, the colors and designs began to acquire symbolic meanings that reflected ideological and political messages. Flags were based on simple shapes and, in most cases, only very simple emblems were used, the most popular being the five-pointed star that was, and remains, a symbol of liberty and independence.

In 1848, political and economic revolutions swept Europe. They started in France, where the people overthrew King Louis Philippe amid demands for universal suffrage, and spread to Germany, Italy, and the Austrian Empire (where the Czechs and Hungarians started demanding independence). These revolutions led many to really believe in the idea of the nation-state and from then on, the need for a national flag became ever more persistent.

In the same way that a coat of arms was linked with a ruler or state, the national flag became a symbol with which people could identify. Often introduced by leaders of independence movements or revolutionaries and then officially adopted by government at a later stage, flags came to symbolize the people as a nation, rather than the actual state. For example, the Union Jack, which has never officially been declared to be the British national flag, provides proof that how people feel toward a flag is far more important than whether legislative action has been taken to incorporate a flag into the constitution.

Almost everywhere in the world, the national flag is held so close to people's hearts that they will risk their lives for it. Under foreign occupation, for example, displaying the national flag has often been an offence punishable by death and yet there have always been people who have been willing to stand up and defiantly hoist their flag as a way of saying, "This is our country, we will not accept interlopers!" On the other hand, a common form of protest against the actions of a foreign country is to publicly burn its national flag. For example, left-wing students in France burnt the German flag when Red Brigade terrorists were arrested. Iranians burnt United States flags under the regime of Ayatollah Khomeini. Polish "Solidarity" trade union workers burnt the European Union flag when they feared they would lose their jobs if Poland joined the EEC. Ironically, burning a flag in a dignified manner is actually considered the best way to dispose of a flag that is no longer in use.

Palestinians burn an Israeli flag over a funeral procession in the Shati refugee camp in Gaza December 16, 2000.

If you think about it, the national flag as the visual symbol of a nation is so deeply ingrained in modern consciousness that often people just use a flag to represent a nation, rather than its name. In the same way, advertisers use pictures of national flags to suggest the international scope of their business, and large hotels eager to attract international clients often display flags of many different nationalities—sometimes, they are even used to indicate the languages spoken by the hotel staff. In most countries, national flags appear on all manner of items, including postage stamps, lapel pins, ties and belt buckles, and souvenir articles including key rings, t-shirts, mugs, umbrellas, and playing cards. And if they're not buying an item covered with their national flag, they are adorning themselves in their own flag: since the early 1990s, the custom of painting the national flag on one's body, at sporting events in particular, has become very popular. People, it seems, just can't get enough of their national flag.

Of course, there are so many more national flags these days than there were in the past, because political changes and developments in the 20th century led to a greater number of countries requiring representation. In 1900, there were 49 sovereign countries. In 2000, there were more than 200. These countries not only adopted a national flag, but numerous government service flags, ensigns and sea flags as well. This means that, on a day to day basis, the flags of the head of state, national and state flags, flags of government agencies and officers, and the flags of political parties will be flying, with the result that there are a lot of countries flying a lot of flags.

Probably the most flag-filled nation in the world is Switzerland. There, at least three flags (the national one, that of the canton, and that of the commune or town) are displayed together, while the larger streets in the cities are decorated with the national flag and the flags of all the cantons. However, Germany probably comes a close second, having national, provincial, and civic flags (mostly in banner form) on permanent display. In the United States and Scandinavian countries, national flag flying is also a popular pastime: you'll find the national flag displayed not only by the authorities and public bodies, but also by a large part of the population in front of private houses.

Aside from coming to play a very important national role in the last few centuries, flags have also come to play a crucial political role. Awareness of this fact has induced totalitarian and oppressive regimes to de-legalize the flags of their opponents and to persecute those who defy the ban. For example, in Spain, when Franco was in power

Like the citizens of the United States, the Norwegians take great pride in their national flag.

between 1939 and 1975, it became illegal to display the Basque flag. In response, the Basque separatists hoisted a booby-trapped flag that blew up when the police tried to remove it. More recently, Israeli authorities have ensured that Palestinians caught with the flag of Palestine are severely punished.

The perceived significance of a flag has also caused problems in countries that are not subjected to oppressive regimes. For example, Germany witnessed a serious and long-lasting conflict soon after the First World War over changes to the national flag. The struggle was between those who wanted to restore the tricolor dating to 1848 and those who wanted to keep the flag designed by Bismarck in 1867. In other words, this was a political conflict between adherents of two different ideologies. The black, red, and gold of the earlier version were perceived as the colors of the democratic republic, representing unity, law, and freedom, while Bismarck's black, white, and red tricolor (incorporating the black and white of Prussia and the red and white of Brandenburg) was a reminder of the glorious days of the empire. The situation became so tense that the republican government decided on a compromise: the 1848 flag was restored as the national flag, while all the sea flags remained black, white, and red, with the addition of the national colors of the canton. When Hitler rose to power in 1933, the German flags were changed again. The black, white, and red tricolor was reinstated as the national flag, but it had to be displayed with the Nazi Party's "Hakenkreuz" flag. Today, the German national flag is the same as the 1848 version.

Flags of Achievement

Emotions certainly run high when a national flag is involved, but sometimes it is for far more positive reasons. For example, at modern sporting events such as international football and rugby matches, teams—pride written all over their faces—stand to attention in front of the national flag and listen to the national

anthem prior to the actual game. Likewise, at the Olympic Games, the national flags of the three athletes on the podium are raised after they have been handed out their medals. These are emotional moments and many a tear has been shed, even by the most hardened of athletes, at the point when the national flag makes its appearance.

Of course, all kinds of flags—not just the national variety—are used frequently in modern sports. For example, flags are used as markers at skiing events; in soccer the referee's assistant carries a flag to indicate when the football has gone out of

US sprinter Michael Johnson holds aloft the Stars and Stripes after winning Olympic gold.

play, and whether it is a goal kick or corner; and flags are placed at the corners of football pitches and to mark cricket boundaries. However, probably the best known flag in sport is the chequered flag used in motor racing, which is used to designate the winner and to close the race—it is waved at the winner, but held still for the runners-up. Flags are also used to signal the beginning and end of major sporting events: think of the opening and closing ceremonies at the 2000 Olympic Games in Sydney and you will recall a sea of flags, some of which will have been the well-known flag of the Olympic Movement dating from 1914 and the flag designed specifically for the Olympic Games.

And, just as ancient civilizations made a habit of planting their flag on the walls of a city following a successful invasion, it has also become a bit of a tradition for the national flag to be symbolically planted in places that are discovered. For example, Roald Amundsen planted the Norwegian flag at the South Pole in 1911; Edmund Hillary and Sherpa Tenzing Norgay placed the flags of New Zealand and Nepal respectively on top of Mount Everest in 1953; and the United States flag was carried to the North Pole by Robert Peary in 1909 and to the moon by Neil Armstrong and Edwin "Buzz" Aldrin in 1969.

In fact, whenever we have something to celebrate these days—be it Christmas, Easter, Halloween, birthdays, the birth of a baby, a Silver Jubilee, or a village fete—flags or, more specifically, bunting is one of the first items out of the cupboard. Bunting, which is actually the name of the material from which the flags are made, consists of lots of mini flags that are either triangular or rectangular in shape and have been strung together for draping across buildings and between trees in gardens. Depending on its usage, it can come in team colors, national colors or neutral shades and, these days, often carries a corporate sponsor's logo or advertising.

Flags, then, have had many varied uses over the years, from the useful to the frivolous.

THE HISTORY OF SEA FLAGS

The history of sea flags is an integral part of general maritime history, because it reflects the political, dynastic, and heraldic developments that took place over the years. Factors such as the evolution of naval tactics, the condition of seaborne trade, and technological advances in ship design and communications have all affected the use of flags at sea.

In the late eighth century, the Vikings were the first Europeans to use sea flags. As they patrolled the northern European waters in their longships, sailing as far as Greenland and North America, they sometimes raided and plundered coastal towns and villages in Britain and France, and, at other times, settled and intermarried with the local people. Mounted in vertical staffs on their ships were their well-known triangular Raven Flags, with their slightly rounded outer edges, while high on the ships' bows were flags that were probably used as vanes to detect wind direction. If you visit the Historiska Museet (Museum of National Antiquities) in Stockholm, you will be able to see a gilded vane dating from the 11th century that has several holes along its curved edge, to which rings with tassels could be attached to replicate the Viking flag.

From the ninth to the 12th centuries, merchant ships that plied their trade on the North and Baltic Seas carried a metal grid cross at the top of their masts as a symbol of the king's protection. From at least the 12th century, princes and cities in the territories dependent on the German Empire used the same symbol, in the form of a staff topped with a cross, on land. Also in the 12th century, a second symbol of the king's protection appeared, which took the shape of a gonfanon (without any emblems) and was attached to a spear or staff topped with a cross. Known as the "vexillo roseum imperiali" or the Blutbanner (Blood

Banner), it was a red banner that the German emperor presented to princes and counts, thus giving them the right of judicial power over life and death in their domains, and obliging them to provide men for the imperial army. Later, the Blutbanner was also awarded to cities that became free imperial cities and to the freed peasants of the Swiss canton of Schwyz.

The oldest sea flag known to exist in the Mediterranean region belongs to Genoa—an illustration dated 1113 shows a white flag with a red cross. A little less than 50 years later, Pisa received the red imperial banner. Although the two flags resemble those of England and the German sea port of Hamburg, they are—in fact—the originals. Not that similarities between flags would have caused confusion at the time, because (even when the flags of England and Hamburg came into existence in the 13th century) merchant ships did not travel such long distances, so an English ship would never have met a vessel from Genoa. Eventually, however, the flags did change in order to be distinctive: Pisa added a distinctive white cross to its imperial banner, while Hamburg added a white shield with a red castle to its red flag.

At the beginning of the 13th century, it became a trend across northern Europe for merchant ships to fasten a single-colored gonfanon to their masts, which were topped with a cross. The gonfanon of the Hanseatic League—a commercial association of European towns that dominated trade between the Atlantic and Baltic—as well as that of Denmark was red, while the English used a white gonfanon. In the second half of the 13th century, in order to set their flags apart, the gonfanons were either divided up into different colored areas or simple emblems were added to them, the most common of which was the Christian cross. For example, the red cross of St. George was added to the English gonfanon. Around the same time, new flags in the shape of banners were placed at the stern, while the mast still carried a gonfanon, although a pennant or banner later replaced that.

A French man-of-war flying the Royal Flag (white, with the arms of France).

It was also at the beginning of the 13th century that England claimed sovereignty over the seas and insisted that all ships belonging to other countries had to salute English ships by lowering their topsails and, later, by striking the flag as well. If captains refused to follow these orders, they were regarded as the enemy and their ships and cargo were forfeited. Surprisingly, the vast majority of foreign ships deferred to England's request, but perhaps this was more to do with the fact that England only insisted on a salute and did not levy duties on ships passing through the English Channel. The practice of acknowledging English ships became obsolete in 1805, but merchant ships salute foreign vessels to this day by dipping the ensign as an act of courtesy. Warships do not dip their ensign to each other, but if a merchant vessel dips to them, then they will reply.

It was at sea that some of the first flags identifying nationality were used. In 1297, King Edward I of England and Guy, Count of Flanders, drew up a legally binding contract that insisted all ships should display flags as identification. In particular, it noted that all merchant ships should "carry in their ensigns or flags the arms of their own ports certifying their belonging to the said ports." This was one of the first times (of which we know) that the word "ensign" had been used to describe a distinguishing flag. Today, it is generally accepted that an ensign is the national flag of a ship—it can also, as in the case of the British ensign—denote the function of the ship. The word ensign derives from the Latin words "insigne" and "signum," which mean signal and sign respectively.

Interesting information on the flags used at sea between the 14th and 16th centuries can be reaped from "portolanos," navigational charts that were produced to meet the practical needs of seamen. They provided a coastal outline with the positions of the cities and ports, together with their flags and banners, but no details of the hinterland were given. Often the flags were very small and their design simplified, but they still contain valuable data.

Up until the 17th century, the merchant ships of the main maritime powers used their national ensigns as a passport to sail to Turkey, North Africa, China, and India. However, all that changed when King Henry VI of France and Sultan Ahmed of the Turkish Empire signed a treaty that lasted from 1604 to 1675, which allowed French ships to visit Turkish ports and trade "under the authorization and security of the Banner of France." A British-Turkish capitulation treaty put an end to those French rights when it reserved the right to free trade in Turkey for the "English nation and the English Merchants and all other nations or Merchants who are or shall come under the banner and protection of England." Similar treaties were made between Western powers and Mediterranean states throughout the second half of the 17th century and into the 18th. One of the purposes of these treaties was to protect commercial shipping from pirates.

These days, international law demands that every ship over a certain size displays its national colors, which means that it should fly its national or mercantile flag or naval ensign. If it doesn't, it's a pirate ship. All merchant ships fly the national flag of the country where they were registered, which is not necessarily the country where they are owned. Flags of convenience are flown by ships registered for reasons of convenience and, perhaps more importantly, economy in countries such as Panama, Liberia, Honduras, Costa Rica, and the

Bahamas. If the national flag of the country where the ship was registered has a complicated crest, a ship will fly a simplified version of the flag. Other flags flown by ships today include signal flags (to send messages to other ship and those on land), company flags (those of the owning company), and courtesy flags (of the country visited).

Sea Flags of Great Britain

In the 14th century, all English ships used the Royal Standard as their national flag. However, by the end of the Middle Ages, the right to use the Royal Standard had been withdrawn, except with special permission. For example, in 1497, when John Cabot set sail on the voyage during which he would find North America, he was allowed to use the Royal Standard.

English ships during the medieval era, particularly those named after a saint, often carried flags with pictures of saints and a coat of arms that contemporary heralds had fancifully ascribed to them. However, Protestant criticism of "superstitious images" in the 1530s and 1540s meant that the majority of these flags disappeared. The only one to survive was the cross of St. George that had been regarded (unofficially at first) as something of a national, rather than a religious, emblem since the 14th century.

In the 16th and 17th centuries, the king's ships carried lots of flags. Enormous streamers, measuring up to 60 meters in length, would adorn the main masthead, while smaller streamers were used on the other mastheads. In addition, a number of armorial banners carrying the king's royal arms and badges, as well as the cross of St. George, streamers featuring animals (such as dragons and lions) and lots of small pennants would be used to decorate the ship. At the same time, merchant ships were less flamboyant in their flag display than the king's ships—they would put bunting out on special occasions, but under normal circumstances all they displayed was a square flag with the St. George's cross.

Just as today a flag of command is hoisted when the flag officer, rank of rear admiral or above, is aboard, from the reign of Henry VIII (1509–47), flags were used to mark out the flagship of the commander-in-chief of a fleet. And, toward the end of his reign, more sophisticated tactics were introduced, which included dividing the fleet into squadrons distinguished by the position of their masthead flags, with each flagship having an extra flag.

From the reign of Queen Elizabeth I (1558–1603), English sea flags tended to be geometric or heraldic in style, rather

A ship during the reign of King Henry VIII with its complicated arrangement of flags.

than displaying representations of saints or beasts—unless, of course, they were part of the heraldic arms. During Good Queen Bess's reign, and that of her successor James I, the striped ensign, which developed from the striped deck level flags used on the ships of Henry VIII's navy, was often used. By the end of the 16th century, striped ensigns were common throughout Europe, with those flown on English ships carrying the cross of St. George in the canton. The colors of the stripes do not appear to have been important, although red and white (the colors of the St. George cross) were very popular. When Queen Elizabeth sent her fleet against the Spanish Armada in 1588, contemporary accounts mention that each ship carried an ensign, the flag of St. George and (most) had streamers.

House flags of shipping companies can be traced to the late 16th and early 17th centuries. Some of the great trading companies, such as the Royal Africa Company, used distinctive flags—its jack, for example, was a cross of St. George within a double border of red and white chequers. Meanwhile, the East India Company had a red and white striped house flag that typically featured 13 stripes with the cross of St. George in the canton. The East India Company continued to use this house flag in Eastern waters and beyond St. Helena in the Atlantic even after 1674, when a proclamation stipulated that merchant ships should use the red ensign.

In 1603, when James VI of Scotland became James I of England and brought about the permanent union of the two countries, the Royal Standard—which since the early 15th century had borne three gold fleurs-de-lis on blue representing the English crown's claim to France and three gold lions on red for England—was changed to include the lion of Scotland. Later, when Ireland joined the Union, the harp would also be added. Interestingly, Wales was, and remains, a principality belonging to the Prince of Wales and has, therefore, never been represented on the British Royal Standard or Union Flag.

In 1606, the design of the "British" or "Union" Flag caused upset in Scotland because the English cross had precedence over the Scottish cross. Originally designed for general use at sea, in 1634, Charles I restricted usage of the Union Flag to the king's own ships. English ships, therefore, reverted to flying the St. George cross, while Scottish ships flew that of St. Andrew. All this was an attempt by Charles I to restore the power of the Royal Navy. Since the Middle Ages, England had claimed sovereignty over the English Channel and all foreign ships were supposed to observe this sovereignty by lowering their flags and topsails in salute to a ship of the English Crown. Charles I, who was eager to ensure this "right," therefore decided to make a visible distinction between English Navy and merchant ships. Thus it has been illegal ever since 1634 for ships other than those in the English Navy to fly the Union Flag without special permission. Flown on a jack staff at the bow of Navy ships, it became known as the Union Jack. Instead of the Union Flag, non-Navy ships were told to fly one of three plain-colored ensigns—red, white, and blue—that had the cross of St. George in the canton. These ensigns are still in use today.

During the reign of Charles I, naval fleet tactics were still experimental and flag arrangements varied, but large fleets of warships were sometimes divided into three squadrons: the center commanded by the Admiral of the Fleet, the "van" by the Vice-Admiral, and the rear by the Rear-Admiral. The three squadrons would be assigned different colors, usually red, blue, and white in that order of seniority.

During the years of the Commonwealth (1649–60), the English sea flags were constantly changing. The Royal Standard and Union Flag obviously disappeared altogether, but—on Charles II's succession to the throne—all the flags that had

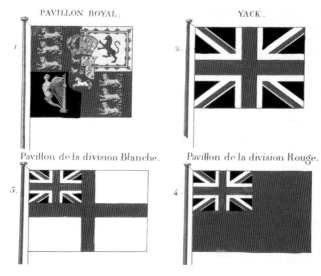

British maritime flags of the 19th century.

been used pre-1649 were restored. The arrangement of large fleets of warships now settled into a pattern, which was maintained for 200 years; there were still three squadrons, but the seniority of the colors flown changed to red, white, then blue, in addition to which they all flew the Union Jack. The rank of the officer in command was determined by what flag was flown where.

The history of British sea flags other than those in the Royal Navy is not as well documented as naval flags, but one area of concern from around this time was the prevention of unauthorized use of flags reserved for the navy. As we

HMS Warrior *flying the red ensign.*

already know, in the early 17th century, some merchant ships flew striped ensigns similar to those used by the king's ships. A 1606 proclamation, however, stated that all privately owned ships must fly the Union Flag on the main and the St. George's cross on the fore, and these remained the "correct" flags until 1634. It was then that Charles I decided that the Union Flag was to be used by the king's ships only and restricted merchant ships to using the St. George's cross only. Not that the merchant ships necessarily obeyed orders. Many kept flying the Union Flag for a number of reasons, including exemption from port duties in France and the fact that it negated the need for a pilot in Holland. Various proclamations up to 1707 re-stated the king's wish and, eventually, the red ensign with the St. George's cross at the stern and the St. George's jack came into general use.

Officially, the red ensign has been legal for British merchant ships since 1674, with the blue ensign being reserved for public vessels and the white one for yachts. However, some merchant ships in the last century or so have used the blue ensign, because the captain and/or some of crew have been members of the Royal Naval Reserve. For example, *Titanic* hoisted a blue ensign for this very reason.

Prior to 1694, there was nothing to differentiate between the navy's warships and vessels in the "civil departments" of the navy or other branches of the king's service, such as transport and victualling offices—the Union Jack was used by all. In 1694, however, it was decided that public service vessels would fly a red jack with the Union Flag in a large canton and the badge of the department in the fly. For example, the Ordnance Board placed a shield with three field guns in the fly. In 1864, however, that all changed and new flag arrangements were introduced. The ensigns of public office ships became blue with the Union Flag in the canton and the badge in the fly, and these remain the regulation colors for "vessels employed in the service of any public office in the United Kingdom" to this day.

Privateers (or "private men of war") owned their own ships, which carried "letters of marque" from the Crown that licensed them to raid enemy commerce and take prizes, and their flags had much in common with those flown on the sovereign's ships. For example, Sir Francis Drake and Sir John Hawkins were two of the most famous privateers active during Queen Elizabeth I's reign. In the 17th century, despite the proclamation of 1634, privateers continued to use the King's Jack whether or not they had special warrant to do so and tended to make themselves look like naval vessels. Official efforts to stop them were ineffective. A proclamation in 1694 introduced a special "privateer's jack" in which the Union Flag appeared as a large canton in a red field (just like those flown on public office

The typical skull and crossbones flag of pirate ships was designed to strike fear into the hearts of sailors.

ships). This jack, and the red ensign, remained the official colors of a British privateer until privateering was abolished in 1856, but privateers still continued to use the Union Jack and naval pennant well into the 18th century.

There was much change on the flag front as the 17th century came to a close and the 18th began. As the main enemy of Britain at that time was France, it was difficult to distinguish the white English ensign from the white flags of the French navy, so, from 1702, a broad cross of St. George was added to the white ensign. In the same year, the Lord High Admiral lost the right to fly the Royal Standard, and its usage became restricted to ships that had the sovereign on board. It is still used today, along with the Union Jack and the anchor flag (a badge for the Lord High Admiral that originated early in the 17th century), by the Queen, who is, of course, her own High Admiral.

In 1707, following the Act of Union, the Union Jack replaced the cross of St. George in the canton of the ensigns. In the following century or so, there were no important changes in the design of the main command flags and colors of the British Navy. However, from the 18th century merchant ships were banned from flying pennants and used short vanes, usually red, instead.

The 18th century also saw the origin of the individual company house flag, rather than the ensign of the East India Company. In 1771, a signal station was erected on Bidston Hill, Liverpool, and ships would raise the owner's distinguishing flag as they approached, so that those based in the company offices on land would be prepared to receive the ship. House flags, which were traditionally flown from the main mast, became fairly common after the Napoleonic Wars (1799–1815) and pretty much universal by the mid-19th century. During the early days of steam navigation, merchant ships were also distinguished by markings on their funnel, which might or might not be related to the design of the house flag.

The 17th and 18th centuries are generally accepted as the golden age of piracy. Pirate ships flew either plain flags with a generally understood color symbolism (black representing death or red representing battle, danger, or blood) or more individual and flamboyant flags that bore various symbols of death—it was the latter that came to be known by the term "Jolly Roger" early in the 18th century. However, the 20th century revival version with which we are familiar, in other words the skull and crossbones, is over simplified. In the 17th and 18th centuries, a Jolly Roger would have been a portraiture of death, with an hour glass in one hand and a dart in the other, at the end of which would be a bleeding heart.

On January 1, 1801, when the United Kingdom of Britain and Ireland came into existence, Ireland came to be represented by the cross of St. Patrick (a red saltire on a white field) in the Union Flag and, therefore, on the ensigns.

Since the early 19th century, some of the earliest yacht clubs have had special dispensation to use ensigns other than the standard red. For example, members of the Yacht Club (which was formed at Cowes in 1815, became the Royal Yacht Club in 1820 and, finally, the Royal Yacht Squadron in 1833) have legally used a version of the white ensign without the large cross of St. George since 1829. Subsequently, other clubs were given the same right, but all except the Royal Yacht Squadron had this special privilege withdrawn in 1842 and members' vessels remain the only ones outside the Royal Navy that are allowed to use the white ensign. However, other clubs have the right to use specially defaced red and blue ensigns, or the plain blue ensign. Other flags used by British yachts are the burgee (the flag of the club, which is usually triangular); the personal flag of the owner (which is usually rectangular); and the flags or broad pennants of "flag officers" of yacht clubs, private racing flags, and prize flags indicating races that have been won.

By the 19th century, the tactical division of fleets into three squadrons was more or less obsolete. Horatio Nelson's decision to order his fleet to wear ensigns of a single color demonstrates that the distinction of ships by squadronal color had ceased to be useful. In 1864, the system was abolished completely and the Royal Navy adopted the white ensign. The blue ensign was set aside for ships in public service and the red ensign for privately owned ships. From the mid-19th century, it became customary for British merchant ships to use as a jack a version of the Union Jack with white border, and this is still a legally permitted jack.

By the 1870s, steamships were coming into use and, not having masts, a new system was needed to help differentiate the officer in command and it remains in use today. So, for example, vice admirals have a small red ball in the upper hoist of the admiral's flag.

Sea Flags of the US

The early British settlers on the east coast of America used British flags both on land and sea. For example, in the 1630s, when a red ensign with a cross of St. George in the canton was the flag used by most English ships, it was also in military use in Massachusetts. The only officially authorized special flag for colonial ships was a short-lived variant of the Union Flag, which had a white shield placed in its center. Established in 1701 as a jack for ships commissioned by colonial governors for official business, there is no evidence that it was ever widely used.

It was not until the political ferment of the American Revolution took hold that a wide range of new flags were put into use. In 1775, the first collective flag of the colonies called the "Continental Colors" was created and it was ceremonially hoisted by George Washington on Prospect Hill, Somerville, Massachusetts on January 1, 1776. Also known (less correctly) as the Great Union Flag and Cambridge Flag, it had a Union Flag in the canton, while the field bore seven red and six white stripes. It was sheer coincidence that the East India Company ships used something similar at the time, as the 13 stripes were used to represent the 13 colonies and the Union Flag showed allegiance to the British Crown.

When the Declaration of Independence was made on July 4, 1776, a new flag was needed. Almost a year later,

The early American flag known as the "Continental Colors."

on June 14, 1777, Congress decreed the existence of the Stars and Stripes. However, the flag was not universally adopted at once. For example, vessels of war on the State of Massachusetts Bay sometimes placed a pine tree over the stripes, and sometimes the stripes were red, white, and blue, not just red and white. Some ships even flew red and white or red, white, and blue striped ensigns with no canton. However, by the early 19th century, the stars on a blue background in the canton and red and white stripes in the field had become universal on American ships, both naval and merchant. Early flag resolutions of Congress did not stipulate precise propositions or details of design, so American shipowners in the 19th century amused themselves by arranging the stars in different formations, such as an anchor, their own initials or the letters US. It was not until 1912 that precise proportions and detailed arrangements were defined.

Subsequently, sea flags followed alterations of the stars and stripes as new states joined. The Stars and Bars, first flag of the Confederate Southern States in the American Civil War, adopted in March 1861, was used on land and at sea as an ensign.

Since the beginning of the 19th century, there's been no distinction between the naval and merchant ensigns in the US. As was traditional in the Royal Navy of Great Britain, the distinguishing flags of a ship in the US Navy are the jack, which has been—since at least 1785—a flag of the starry canton (or Union) of the stars and stripes, and the commissioning pennant, which consists of a blue hoist with a row of seven white stars, and a fly divided red over white. The pennant was standardized in this form in 1934.

Signaling

One of the oldest uses of flags is for signaling at sea. For example, vexilloids were used by both the Greeks and Persians when they were at war (547–478 BC) and, by the Middle Ages, both the Genoese and Venetian fleets had developed a more elaborate signal system. From then, until the invention of radio in the early 20th century, flags were the only method of communication between ships out of hailing distance of one another and between ship and shore.

The first specially made signal flag used by the English fleet was the "Banner of the Council," which was introduced in 1369 to summon captains to the Admiral's ship. However, there were certain internationally understood conventions, such as a red flag (representing blood and defiance) that was used for battle and a white flag that stood for a truce. It was the three Dutch wars that took place in the second half of the 17th century that spurred on the need for greater communication between ships. Flags from this time were used to send tactical messages between ships—previous battle tactics had not been any more complicated than proceed into battle or retreat. In 1673, the first printed volume of "Sailing and Fighting Instructions" was issued by James, Duke of York, Lord High Admiral. It detailed how the Admiral could convey various orders to his fleet by hoisting flags (some standard, some used solely for signaling) in different positions.

These "Instructions" were revised and extended until 1703, when they were superseded by the "Instructions for the Directing and Governing Her Majesty's Fleet in Sailing and Fighting"—a manual that was to remain in use until the 1780s. In between, more and more instructions were added to the repertoire, with a corresponding increase in the number of special signal flags required. The only problem with this type of signaling was that it was a one-way method of communication: only the fleet's flagship carried a full set of signaling flags, so that the admiral could convey orders to his fleet.

In 1776, Admiral Lord Howe took the first step to a new approach when he published a new book entitled "Signal Book for the Ships of War," which revised and simplified the range of flags used for signaling. In other words, a smaller number of signal flags were used to create a greater range of signals. Fourteen years later, Howe revised his approach by adopting a numerary system that had ten basic flags, which had the same meaning wherever they were hoisted on the ship. According to this new system, the flags were read from the top down, so the signal for No.53 "prepare for battle" involved flag No.5 hoisted above flag No.3. What's more, the flags were smaller than previous signal flags and were very simple so that they could be easily distinguished. For example, flag No.5 is quartered red and white, while No.3 is divided vertically blue/white/blue. The only shortcoming of Howe's system was that only those signals listed in the "Signal Book" could be made. Still, the system—or variations of it—stayed in use until around 1800.

It was in 1812 that Captain Sir Home Popham created "Telegraphic Signals or Marine Vocabulary," a system by which he gave each letter of the alphabet a number, so that words not in the signal book could be spelt out. It was using Popham's code that enabled Horatio Nelson to "speak" those famous words: "England expects every man will do his duty." With modifications, Popham's system remained crucial to British naval signaling until well into the 20th century. However, since the mid-19th century, flag signaling has yielded much of its importance to signaling methods based on semaphore machines, hand semaphore, flashing lamps, and, most recently, radio.

As far as merchant codes are concerned, the East India Company had its own signaling system in the 18th century, but there was no generally accepted language between merchant ships, except for certain conventions, such as hoisting an ensign upside-down to indicate distress. Captain Frederick Marryat of the Royal Navy, who produced the "Code of Signals for the Merchant Service," filled this

The semaphore flags that Admiral Nelson used to signal his famous message to the fleet.

gap in 1817. Like Popham's, it was a numerary-based system, with ten basic numeral flags. A huge international success, it was continuously revised and re-printed, and the 12th edition published in 1854 was renamed the "Universal Code of Signals."

However, in 1857, the "Commercial Code of Signals" (known as the International Code from about 1870) was introduced and superseded Marryat's version. Employing 18 flags and including 70,000 signals, it has been constantly updated and improved since it was created. As well as signifying a letter of the alphabet, each flag has a complete meaning of its own, some of which have very traditional meanings. For example, the "Blue Peter," a blue flag with a white rectangle in its center, which is "P" in the code, also means (when a ship is in port) that "all persons report on board, vessel about to proceed to sea." It has been recorded with more or less the same meaning since about the 1750s.

To this day, seamen still have to learn the correct method of hoisting the flags and how to interpret signals despite technological advances, but their usage is decreasing. In fact, signal flags are most often used these days to "dress up" ships: the custom of putting out all the flags for a special occasion that dates to the 16th century.

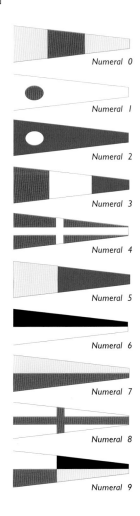

Numeral 0

Numeral 1

Numeral 2

Numeral 3

Numeral 4

Numeral 5

Numeral 6

Numeral 7

Numeral 8

Numeral 9

Alpha

Beta

Charlie

Delta

Echo

Foxtrot

Golf

Hotel

India

Juliet

Kilo

Lima

Mike

November

Oscar

Papa

Quebec

Romeo

Sierra

Tango

Uniform

Victor

Whiskey

X-Ray

Yankee

Zulu

1st-substitute

2nd-substitute

3rd-substitute

THE STORIES BEHIND KEY FLAGS

Flick through the gazetteer at the end of this book, where every national flag is reproduced, and you will see that every flag is unique and yet many of them are also very similar. This is hardly a case of coincidence.

Countries in certain parts of the world, for example South America, often have similar designs because they have a shared history. The flag used by Venezuelan revolutionary Francisco de Miranda in the early 19th century came to symbolize South and Central American emancipation from Spanish rule and was subsequently the basis for three national flags—those of Colombia, Venezuela, and, later, Ecuador. The colors used were blue (representing the Atlantic Ocean), which separated the red (of Spain) from the yellow (wealth of the Americas).

In other parts of the world—and not necessarily those that are geographically close—countries may have similar national flags because they are linked by specific traditions or interests, or because a country is modeled on another that it admires for political or religious reasons. In this way, we will see later in this chapter how Christian and Muslim countries often have striking similarities in their flags, as do those whose governments have shared Communist beliefs.

Of course, there is another reason why flags are alike and that is related to history. National flags did not develop on a large scale until the 19th century, which means that of all the flags still in use by countries today, only 12 were adopted prior to 1800. These flags, therefore, and in particular those of Denmark, Great Britain, the Netherlands, Russia, the United States, France, and Turkey, have played a crucial role in influencing the designs and colors of more recent national flags.

For all these reasons, it is possible to group the entire world's flags into a series of "flag families," although some flags may end up belonging to more than one. For example, there are certain flags that display the white, black, and green pan-Arab colors, as well as the Muslim crescent or star—the national flag of Iraq is a good example. And there are those that bear both the red, white, and blue of the French tricolor, as well as the Christian symbol of the cross: the flag of the Dominican Republic is one.

Finally, though, it is worth remembering that however many similarities the flags of the world display, each is unique and designed to stimulate people in a particular way, because it represents the existence, origin, authority, possession, loyalty, glory, beliefs, objectives, and status of an entire nation. Flags are used to honor and dishonor, warn and encourage, threaten and promise, exalt and condemn, commemorate and deny, and they incite the child in school, the soldier, the voter, the enemy, the ally, and the stranger. In fact, men and women are willing to fight and even die for these pieces of colored cloth: that is how much importance they attach to a national flag.

The Christian Cross

Among ancient civilizations in communities as diverse as Mesopotamia, China, Scandinavia, and Greece, the cross was considered a magical sign and decorative motif, but in the modern world it is universally recognized as the symbol of Christianity.

In the first few centuries after Christ's death, the main Christian symbol was a fish, which was often accompanied by the Greek letters that spell out the word "fish." Acrostically, these letters mean "Jesus Christ God's Son Saviour." However, in the third century, Christian communities began to use cross-like emblems, such as an anchor with a crosspiece or a human figure with outstretched arms, which was undoubtedly linked with the discovery of the cross on which Christ was crucified. Gradually, the cross became a symbol of martyrdom, resurrection, redemption, and salvation.

From the ninth century to the end of the 12th century, a metal cross at the top of a mast was the only emblem marking out merchant ships in northern Europe. Later, the cross became the most common charge on the merchant ensigns used by cities and nations across Europe. Many chose to use the cross of their patron saint—that was certainly the case in Denmark and England—no doubt hoping that this would provide protection against the maritime elements. These ensigns would then go on to become the national flags of many of the nations.

Portugal and the kingdom of Jerusalem have the oldest flags bearing a cross known to man. In the 12th century, the Portuguese flag bore a blue cross on a white field. Later, the white field carried a cross made of five blue shields—an arrangement that remains in the center of the coat of arms of Portugal to this very day. Meanwhile, the 12th century flag of the kingdom of Jerusalem displayed five golden yellow crosses on a white field.

In the 13th and 14th centuries, the flags of the Teutonic Order, France, Savoy, Malta, Barcelona, and Constantinople were all charged with a simple cross, although those of Barcelona and Constantinople displayed additional devices. In the 17th and 18th centuries, a white cross on a blue field constituted the civil ensign of France; and those of several French provinces (including Provence and Picardy) and ports (such as Marseilles and Calais) also bore a cross. Such widespread use of the cross in the Mediterranean was to influence the flags of some of the nations created in the 19th and 20th centuries: the Greek flag bears a cross to this day.

Until the end of the 14th century, the cross was totally symmetrical, the center of the cross corresponding with the center of the field. However, the people of Denmark changed all that when they positioned their cross to the left

The "Dannebrog" flies from the stern of a boat in a Danish harbor.

of the center, with the result that the arms of the cross formed squares in the hoist and rectangles in the fly. The Danish flag, known as the "Dannebrog" (literally meaning Danish cloth) is, in fact, the oldest national flag, and one of the oldest flags in use. There are two stories regarding its origin. According to legend, the red flag with a white cross fell from heaven in 1219, during a battle at which the Christian Danes were victorious over the pagan Estonians, but according to historical records, the flag first appeared in the arms of King Valdemar Atterdag in the 14th century.

Over the years, the example of the Danish flag has been followed by all the Scandinavian countries (as well as by Normandy—a reminder that the Norsemen once colonized parts of Europe) and a large sub-family, called the Scandinavian cross, has thus come into being. Even Finland, which is not a truly Scandinavian country, deliberately chose a Scandinavian cross in 1918, because it wanted to proclaim solidarity with Sweden, Norway, and Denmark, rather than Russia.

As well as the standard variety, there are some more elaborate versions of the Christian cross on flags around the world. For example, the Swiss flag carries a stunted white cross on a red field that first appeared on the flag of the canton of Schwyz and on the red schwenkels of other cantons in the 13th century. And the flag of Malta bears the George Cross, which was awarded to the country in 1943 by King George VI, to mark the heroism of the Maltese under daily bombing by the Germans and Italians during the Second World War.

It is not just in Europe that the Christian cross has made an appearance on national flags and ensigns. It was once placed in the canton of the Liberian flag, and currently plays an important part in the flags of such far-flung nations as Dominica, the Dominican Republic, and Tonga.

The Muslim Crescent

The crescent, and sometimes the star as well, are now recognized as the emblems of many Muslim countries, but this has not always been the case. The crescent, which is one of the oldest symbols known to humanity, first appeared (along with the sun) on seals created in Mesopotamia as early as 2300 BC. And from at least the second millennium BC, it was the symbol of the Mesopotamian moon gods Nanna in Sumer and Sin in Babylonia.

Then, in 339 BC, the crescent became a symbol of Constantinople following a siege of the city by Philip of Macedon, who was the father of Alexander the Great. According to legend, Philip lay siege to Byzantium in 339 BC, but was continually repulsed. As a last resort, he tried to undermine the walls, but because the crescent moon shone so brightly the attempt was discovered and the city was saved from defeat. As a token of their gratitude, the Byzantines adopted the crescent as their badge and Artemis (who was also known as Diana), the goddess of the moon, as their patroness.

Men raising the flag of Pakistan, featuring the Muslim Crescent.

More recently, it is known that the Phoenicians had transplanted the crescent as far as Carthage (now in

Tunisia) by the ninth century. Three hundred years later, the crescent symbol, which is mentioned in the 53rd "surah" (chapter) of the Koran, was adopted by the Turks and soon after it became the main symbol of Islam. However, stars did not appear on Moslem flags until comparatively recently, and there is little evidence that they were used in conjunction with crescents prior to the 18th century. In fact, they were previously considered more of a Western heraldic device, having been used, for example, by King Richard the Lionheart in the late 12th century.

The oldest representations of flags bearing the crescent are depicted on "portolanos," 14th century navigational charts, which may not be accurate illustrations of the original flags, but at least confirm the widespread use of the crescent on flags in the region at that time. Some of the flags featured include those of the kings of Damascus and Lucha (yellow with a white crescent); Cairo (white with a blue crescent); Mahdia in Tunisia (white with a purple crescent); Tunis (white with a black crescent); and the Ottoman Empire (red with one or two crescents). The latter differed later, bearing three white crescents between the 16th and 18th centuries, and just one crescent and an eight-pointed white star from 1793. When the Ottoman Empire finally collapsed, it became the national flag of Turkey, although the star was changed so that it now only has five points. However, having been a world power, the flag has been very important in popularizing the crescent and star on Muslim flags throughout Africa and Asia. For example, when Muhammed Ali, who became Pasha of Egypt in 1805, introduced the first national flag of Egypt, it was red with three white crescents, each accompanied by a white star.

During the last 200 years, the crescent and star have featured on the flags of a number of other Arab countries in North Africa and the Middle East, and those that maintain these features up until the present day include Tunisia, Algeria, Singapore, and the Comoros.

The pan-Arab Countries

As mentioned earlier, some flags—like that of Iraq—combine the Muslim crescent with the pan-Arab colors, which are currently black, white, red, and green, although they have not always been used together in this combination.

The early Arab flags were often only made up of just one color, which was charged with religious inscriptions. Initially, the favored colors were black and white, which were the colors of the two flags ascribed to the Prophet Muhammad. White was chosen because it was the color of the Omayyads, the Muslim dynasty that immediately succeeded the Prophet and was an influential part of the Quraish tribe to which he belonged—they ruled the Muslim Empire from AD 661 to 750, and were Muslim rulers of Spain from AD 756 to 1031. Black was used because it was the color of the Abbasid dynasty, which overthrew the Umayyads and ruled the Muslim Empire from AD 750 to 1258.

Green, which has long been perceived as the color of Islam, was the traditional color of the Fatimids, who were the leaders of the secret Ismaili sect and claimed descent from Fatima, the daughter of the Prophet Muhammad. Red, on the other hand, is the color of the Hashemites, who were the descendants of Hashim (the great-grandfather of the Prophet Muhammad) and were the

A young Kuwaiti boy with his national flag of black, red, white, and green.

75

hereditary amirs of Mecca for centuries. The founder of the modern Hashemite dynasty was Husayn ibn Ali, the amir of Mecca, King of Hejaz (1916–24) and grandfather of the present king of Jordan.

However, it was not until a group of young Arabs met in the Literary Club in Istanbul in 1911 to choose a design for a modern Arab flag that all four colors—white, black, green, and red—were officially agreed as Arab colors. The poet Safi al-Din al-Hili explained why each color had been chosen, when he said: "White are our deeds, black are our battles, green are our fields, red are our knives." Three years later, the central committee of the Young Arab Society in Beirut declared that the flag of any future independent Arab state would be white, black, and green, thereby displaying the colors of the Umayyads, Abbasids, and Fatimids, respectively.

Subsequently, the first flag to be adopted into the Arab flag family was that of Syria in March 1920; a year later, Iraq's was the second. Syria decided to use one white star, while Iraq adopted two, thereby making the point that they were the first and second state to emanate from the "mother-state." The designs of these flags were later modified, but the four pan-Arab colors were retained. Other countries that have adopted the pan-Arab colors include Kuwait (1961) and the United Arab Emirates (1971).

Egypt following the 1952 revolution, during which the monarchy was abolished, introduced a second generation of pan-Arab colors. The revolutionaries introduced the Arab Liberation Flag, a horizontal tricolor composed of black (symbolizing the period of oppression), red (the bloody struggle), and white (a bright future). In the center, an eagle—said to have been the badge of the 12th century Muslim hero Saladin—was introduced. This flag inspired the flags of several Arab nations that chose the republican political system, including those of the Yemen (1962), Syria and Iraq (1963), South Yemen (1967), Libya (1969), and Sudan (1970).

The pan-African Colors

Just as there is a family of flags displaying pan-Arab colors, there is also a family of flags bearing pan-African colors. The two greatest influences on this flag family have been the red, black, and green flag designed by black activist Marcus Garvey in 1917, and the green, yellow, and red flag of Ethiopia, the oldest independent state in Africa.

Garvey organized the first important black unification movement in the United States and sought a new home for black people in Africa. His movement, which was officially called the United Negro Movement Association, was popular in the United States in the 1920s, then spread to the West Indies (particularly Jamaica) and finally across to Africa. Although he created his flag to represent the movement, he eventually wanted it to become the national flag of the unified black state he dreamt of creating.

The colors of the Ethiopian flag date to 1897, when they were chosen for the following reasons: the green to symbolize the land and hope, the yellow to stand for the church, peace, and love, and the red to represent power and faith. When Haile Selassie (otherwise known as Ras Tafari) succeeded to the Ethiopian throne in 1930, supporters of Garvey's movement considered him something of a Messiah and Ethiopia was seen as the promised land. These people, who gained the name Rastafarians, adopted the Ethiopian colors and added black from the Garvey flag, often in the form of a lion, to create their own flag. All the colors have since been used widely in Africa.

In 1957, for example, Ghana became the first independent country in western Africa to adopt a flag that combined the colors of the Ethiopian flag and those of Garvey. Inspired by the flag of the Black Star Line shipping company established by Garvey in Accra, it has green, yellow, and red horizontal stripes and a black star in its center. A year later, Guinea followed suit, adopting red, yellow, and green vertical stripes. Other countries that have subsequently adopted flags displaying three or more of the pan-African colors are Senegal (1960), Mali (1961), Rwanda (1961), Zambia (1964), Guinea Bissau (1973), Sao Tome and Principe (1975), Zimbabwe (1980), Mozambique (1983), Burkina Faso (1984), Congo (1991), and South Africa (1994)—all of these flags are still in use today.

The African countries that only adopted Garvey's colors as their main flag colors are Kenya (1963), Malawi (1964), and Biafra (1967). In all three flags, the black stands for the African people, while the red symbolizes the blood that has been shed in the struggle for independence and the green represents the fertile land.

Flags of International Importance

Some flags simply belong to the world family: they are the flags of international organizations that are instantly recognized by people of every color, creed, and religion, because they never change—the Red Cross flag is the exception to the rule—wherever they are displayed around the world. Among the most famous

are the Olympic flag, with its five circles representing the linking of the five continents in peaceful competition; the United Nations flag, in which peace is personified by olive branches cradling the world; and the Red Cross flag, with a red cross on a white background.

The Olympic flag was designed in 1913 and was first used at the Olympic Games held in Antwerp in 1920. The white represents peace and friendship between the competing nations, while the rings symbolize the five continents and

The Olympic flag with its five symbolically linked circles.

denote the global character of the Olympic movement. During the opening ceremony of every games, a large Olympic flag is raised on a flagpole at the stadium and remains there throughout the event as a reminder of the ideal behind the games: in other words, peace and friendship.

What is now known as the UN flag was created in 1945 by the Graphics Department of the US Office of Strategic Studies (the forerunner of the CIA) as a logo for the first United Nations conference. It is based on a view of the

The internationally recognized flags of the Red Cross. The crescent is used in Muslim countries.

world, as seen from the North Pole, and is encircled by two olive branches that (as well as the color blue) are regarded as a sign of peace. Later the same year, this logo was officially adopted as the UN seal and emblem. The UN itself was established to promote international peace, security, and co-operation. It is the largest and most important international organization, with 185 member states. Its specialized agencies handle international issues including economic, monetary, scientific, educational, social, judicial, and health matters.

The flag of the International Red Cross, which was established in 1863, was suggested by the organization's founder, Swiss philanthropist Henri Dunant. It is the flag of Switzerland, with its colors reversed. For reasons of religious sensitivity, ever since 1876 the Red Cross flag used in Muslim countries has displayed a red Muslim crescent, rather than a cross. The Red Cross monitors the treatment of prisoners of war, and protects civilians during hostilities and natural catastrophes.

The Union Jack & its Family

The Union Jack and the Stars and Stripes are probably the two most famous flags in the world. Although of the two versions currently in use, the Stars and Stripes is actually older than the Union Jack, the origins of the British flag date back much further than the American one.

The English have flown a white flag bearing the red cross of St. George, the country's patron saint, since the middle of the 13th century, if not before. It was one of the flags that they took into battle with them on the Seventh Crusade (1248–54), along with the English royal arms with its heraldic lions and golden fleur de lys. It was also used by merchant and navy ships right up until the early 17th century.

Then, on April 12, 1606, three years after becoming King James I of England and Scotland, a proclamation was issued: "That from henceforth, all our Subjects of this Isle and Kingdome of Great Britaine, and the members thereof, shall beare in their Maintoppe the Red Cross, commonly called S. Georges Crosse, and the White Cross, commonly called S. Andrewes Crosse, joyned together, according to a forme made by our Heralds…" Henceforth, the crosses of St. Andrew and St. George were depicted together as the British flag.

A 12th century reference to the St. Andrew's cross suggests that it dates to the reign of King Hungus in the eighth century: the white saltire certainly seems to have been established much earlier than the red cross of St. George, although the blue background did not become firmly established until the 17th century. By joining forces with the English flag, it was the first step toward what was to become one of the best-known flags in the world. A flag that became well-known thanks to its striking design, the importance of its influence on other flags, and the importance of the British Empire (later known as the Commonwealth) in world history.

Until 1634, the Union Flag was used by every type of British ship, but after that, its use was restricted to the king's own ships or ships in the king's immediate service; English merchant ships were supposed to revert to flying the St. George's cross, while Scottish merchant ships should have been flying the St. Andrew's cross. It was probably at this time that the Union Flag became known as the Union Jack, although—in literal terms—it is only the small flag flown from the jackstaff at the bow of one of the Queen's ships that is a Union Jack. It was also around this period that the merchant ensign, a red flag with the St. George's cross in the canton, was created—it was later legalized in a proclamation of 1674, which also warned merchant vessels that the use of the Union Jack was illegal. Nevertheless, many merchant captains continued to use the "King's jack" in order to gain advantages in foreign waters, such as better protection and exemption from port duties in France.

When England and Scotland formerly became Great Britain in 1707, the Union Jack was placed in the canton of the red, blue, and white ensigns (where formerly either the St. George's cross or St. Andrew's cross had been placed). Subsequently, these red and blue ensigns have been the basis for over 100 colonial and national flags of Commonwealth countries—but more of that later.

When the United Kingdom of Great Britain and Ireland finally came into existence on January 1, 1801, a red saltire (on white) called the cross of St. Patrick was chosen to represent Ireland and was

The Union Jack flying at half-mast over Westminster Abbey on the day of Princess Diana's funeral.

81

incorporated into the Union Flag. Thought to be a 16th century invention based on the Cross of Burgundy, which was used by the Spaniards, it featured in the coat of arms of the Anglo-Irish family of Fitzgerald and was occasionally used as an emblem of Ireland in the 17th century, being adopted as the main emblem of the Order of St. Patrick in 1783. Officially, the red saltire is below the white in the hoist and above it in the fly, so that they are equal in status and therefore do not upset national sensibilities. The Scottish saltire uppermost in the first quarter (the upper hoist) gives slight precedence to Scotland, but turning it upside down changes the precedence in favor of Ireland. This latest version of the Union Flag was subsequently incorporated into the red, white, and blue British ensigns, which thus assumed their modern form.

Meanwhile, the flags of saints George, Andrew, and Patrick remained the flags of England, Scotland, and Ireland respectively. The flag of the fourth country of the United Kingdom, Wales, has never played any part in the Union Jack, because—officially—she is a principality ruled by the Prince of Wales, rather than a country coming directly under the sovereignty of the monarch. Wales does have its own flag, however; it is a red dragon on a green and white field. Today, even though the union with Ireland was dissolved 80 years ago, St. Patrick's cross still remains in the Union Jack, presumably because Northern Ireland is still a part of the United Kingdom.

Interestingly, although Brits always consider the Union Jack as their national flag, it is not. The United Kingdom differs from most other countries in that she has no official national flag. The Union Flag is actually a royal flag for the use of the sovereign and the services and representatives of the sovereign. However, it has twice been stated in Parliament—in 1908 and 1933—that there is no objection to any British subject using the Union Flag ashore—the 1894 Merchant Shipping Act forbids its use afloat. In fact, there are very few specifications regarding the use of the Union Jack. For example, it is usually made in the proportions of 1:2, but that is not essential, and the colors of the flag can be any shade of red and blue—they are not fixed.

It is the British ensign that has really given birth to the family of flags based on the Union Flag. The Colonial Defence Act of 1865 allowed "all vessels belonging to, or permanently in, the service of the Colonies" to use the blue ensign, "with the Seal or Badge of the Colony in the Fly thereof," which made possible the enormous future growth in the number of flags with the Union Jack in the canton. More than 100 colonies used the ensign and some of them, such as Australia, New Zealand, Fiji, and Tuvalu, adopted it—with some alterations, such as Fiji and Tuvalu changing the background color to pale blue—as their national flag on independence.

The British innovation of putting the national flag in the canton of a flag or ensign greatly influenced the merchant ensigns of many countries that did not have formal ties with the British Empire. The example of the striped Elizabethan ensigns induced the Portuguese to adopt a similar ensign in 1640. The blue and red ensigns served as models for the civil ensigns or national flags of Hanover (1801–66), Sardinia (1821–48), Greece (1822–28), China (1928–49), Taiwan (since 1949), Spanish Morocco (1937–56), Samoa (1948–49), the Khmer Republic (1970–75), and flags of the French colonies (see the French Tricolore).

The flag of the United States was one of the first flags to be modeled on the British ensign.

Formally, the civil ensign of a British colony was always, and still is, a plain red ensign. Only a few colonies—Canada (1892), New Zealand (1899), Australia (1903), South Africa (1910), Bermuda (1915), the Isle of Man (1971), Guernsey (1985), the Cayman Islands (1988), and Gibraltar (1996)—obtained the right to deface the red ensign with a badge. What badge they chose to use varied greatly: Gibraltar chose the arms granted to it by King Ferdinand and Queen Isabella of Spain on July 10, 1502, while the golden cross on the civil ensign of Guernsey was the same charge used by William the Conqueror (and had been given to him by the Pope before he embarked on the campaign that ended in victory at the battle of Hastings in 1066). Several British colonies, such as Bermuda, obviously liked the red ensign so much that they introduced a civil ensign in the form of a red flag with the national flag in the canton after gaining independence.

A British Flag Family Example: Australia

The Southern Cross (or Crux), which is one of the world's smallest, but brightest constellations, is visible from the southern hemisphere and has been used for centuries by sailors as a navigational aid. It has, therefore, been a major theme in Australian symbolism since the early 19th century.

The National Colonial Flag of 1823–24 placed the four stars of the Southern Cross on the red St. George's cross of the British white ensign. Less than a decade later, the New South Wales ensign appeared, which was very similar to the Commonwealth Flag at that time, but had stars with eight points—it would later become the Federation Flag. And in 1870, the ensign badge of Victoria also carried a version of the Southern Cross. So it is not really surprising then that the Southern Cross played a major part in the design that won the competition for a flag when Australia became a federal dominion in 1901.

A total of 32,823 designs were entered into the competition in 1900; five separate entrants submitted very similar designs, which were considered the winners, and the flag was officially adopted in February 1903. To this day, the flag consists of the Southern Cross (for Australia) on a blue field with a Union Jack (signifying Australia's links with Britain and the Commonwealth) in the canton. The stars, whose varying numbers of points indicate the brilliance of the actual stars in the sky, are similar to, but not quite the same as, those used in the flag of Victoria. The flag also had a large star of six points representing the six states—the number of points was increased to seven in 1908 when the Northern

Territory of Australia was officially recognized. In 1965, the flag became "The National Flag of Australia": its proportions are set at 1:2, and the red and blue colors have been officially defined. On ships, a red ensign is flown, while the army uses a white ensign.

All seven of Australia's state flags are also based on the blue British ensign and therefore carry the Union Flag in the canton and the state badge (derived from the States' Coats of Arms) in the fly. The oldest of the flags is that from Tasmania, which dates to 1875—the emblem of a Red Lion on a white background represents the historical ties with England

The Australian flag against Sydney skyscrapers.

and has remained pretty much unchanged since the flag's adoption. There is a gold star in each arm and a gold lion at the center of the St. George's cross, which is the badge of New South Wales and was created in 1876. The badge of South Australia, inaugurated in 1904, incorporates a magpie shown with outstretched wings on a yellow background, while Victoria adopted its Southern Cross and crown badge six years later. Queensland chose the Royal Crown at the center of a Maltese cross for its badge when Queen Elizabeth was crowned in 1952 and Western Australia, which adopted its badge the following year, has always used an emblem of a Black Swan since it was founded on the Swan River. The Northern Territory is the exception to the rule: instead of using the blue ensign, its flag depicts the Southern Cross on a black hoist and a black and white stylized Sturt's desert rose on ochre, these being the territorial colors.

At present, the other Australian flag of importance is the Aboriginal land rights flag, which has become a powerful symbol of the native people. Its colors are black, yellow, and red, representing the people, the sun, and the land of Australia, respectively. Should Australia ever become a republic, its flag would undoubtedly change and it is quite likely that the official national colors of Australia—green and yellow—would play a major part in the design of the new flag.

The Stars and Stripes

The Stars and Stripes, along with the Union Jack, has one of the highest international recognition factors of all the flags in existence. However, its exact origins are uncertain, although we can be sure that it evolved gradually and was not the work of just one person.

From the end of the 15th century, North America was colonized by British settlers under the protection of the British flag. They used the red British ensign (both on land and at sea) for the next 100 years or so, which resulted in it playing a significant role in the evolution of the United States national flag, also known as the Stars and Stripes and the Star-spangled Banner.

But exactly how did the Stars and Stripes evolve? We will never know. What we do know is that red, white, and blue were frequently used in flags at the time, and the idea of using stripes to designate states had already been used by the first Dutch colonists of New Amsterdam. They had brought the flag of their homeland with them, and it consisted of seven red and white alternating stripes representing their seven united provinces, which had finally gained freedom from Spain. In addition, the British East India Company, which had been very active in opening up American frontiers, used a flag with stripes, the number of which varied between five and 15.

The rest of the facts, as we know them, are these. The first American sea flag, a merchant ensign consisting of 13 red and white stripes, was introduced in 1775. (The fact that it was identical to some of the flags flown by the British East India Company is probably coincidental.) In December of the same year, the first American flag, known as the Cambridge or Grand Union flag, was created. In the field were 13 red and white stripes (taken from the ensign), which represented the 13 original colonies united in defence of their liberties. In the canton was a Union Jack, symbolising the link with the colonists' mother country of Britain—this was meant to act as a plea for reconciliation, because the colonists were reluctant to defy and break entirely from the mother country at this stage.

When George Washington raised the Grand Union flag for the first time on Prospect Hill at Somerville, Massachusetts on January 1, 1776 (the day that the colonies were declared in rebellion by King George III of England), it immediately became the banner of his Continental Army, hence its other name of the Continental Colors.

Six months later, the Grand Union flag was suspended on the colonies' declaration of independence (July 4, 1776), and, almost a year after the Declaration of Independence, Americans finally replaced the Union Jack with the following words in the law of June 14, 1777: "Resolved, That the Flag of the United States be 13 stripes alternate red and white, that the Union be 13 stars white in a blue field representing a new constellation." It is this day that is commemorated as Flag Day in the United States. However, some circumstances indicate that the Union Jack had already been replaced by the star-filled canton in 1776, and that the Continental Congress's Resolution only confirmed the design already in use—a theory that could be substantiated by the terse wording of the resolution.

So a flag, bearing 13 red and white stripes and a blue canton with 13 white stars came into existence—and although it was not the final version of the Stars and Stripes, it was close to it. Given that the final version of the Union Jack was only created in 1801, when the union with Ireland was formalized and the St. Patrick's red cross added, means that the Star Spangled Banner is actually older than the Union Flag. The idea for the blue canton, the size of which was not specified, may have been copied from the Rhode Island Regiment's "Hope" flag, while the stars were a revolutionary American invention—although the Stars and Stripes was the first national flag to use them, they have been widely copied since, by countries as diverse as the Soloman Islands, Venezuela, and Liberia. As the arrangement of the stars was not fixed, several different designs date from this time. Originally, it seems to have been popular to place the 13 stars in a circle, so that no one star (and therefore state) was given precedence or preference over another. Later, the stars were arranged in parallel staggered rows.

Betsy Ross and the legendary first Stars and Stripes.

Folklore credits Elizabeth "Betsy" Ross of Philadelphia, an upholsterer turned flag maker, with creating this flag, but it seems unlikely. Another myth links the "creation" of the Stars and Stripes with some ladies from Portsmouth, New Hampshire, who are said to have made a Stars and Stripes from their ballroom dresses for Captain John Paul Jones to fly on his ship in July 1777. Others think Francis Hopkinson, a New Jersey judge and signer of the Declaration of Independence, who served two years as chairman of the Navy Board might have had something to do with the design—there is certainly evidence in the form of an invoice that he did do some flag work for the Admiralty Board. It also seems likely that at least some of the inspiration for the flag came from the Washington family coat of arms, which featured red and white stripes and red stars.

Alfred B. Street produced one of the earliest accounts of the symbolism of the flag in October 1777, when he witnessed the flag at the surrender of the British General Burgoyne at Saratoga: "The stars were disposed in a circle, symbolizing the perpetuity of the Union; the ring, like the circling serpent of the Egyptians, signifying eternity. The 13 stripes showed with the stars the number of the United Colonies, and denoted the subordination of the States to the Union, as well as equality among themselves."

After its inauguration, the growth of the Union posed the question of how the new states should be represented in the flag. Originally, the flag was changed to reflect increases in the number of constituent parts of the country. For example, on January 13, 1794, after Vermont (1791) and Kentucky (1792) joined the union, Congress changed the flag so that it had 15 stars and 15 stripes—it remained this way for the next 14 years. It was this version that was made by Mary Pickersgill in Baltimore's Flag House and flew over Fort McHenry, inspiring Francis Scott Key to nickname the flag "the Star Spangled Banner" in a poem, the words of which were recognized as those of the national anthem in 1931.

The Stars and Stripes reflected in the Vietnam Memorial.

When five more states joined the Union between 1796 and 1817, the flag became obsolete and some foresighted members of government realized that adding a stripe for every new member state was not going to work. Peter H. Wendover (1768–1834), representative for New York City, pretty much made it his life work to ensure that the flag was workable. He consulted Captain Samuel Chester Reid, a young sea captain and hero of the 1812 War with no artistic training, who has been pinpointed as the man who came up with the final version of the Stars and Stripes. When asked to produce a lasting design for the national flag, Reid and his wife produced a flag with 13 red and white stripes and a blue field, to which white (state) stars could be added as necessary.

Congress approved the design and President James Monroe signed the act making the flag official on April 4, 1818. It was then that the number of stars was increased to 20 (to accommodate those states that had joined between 1796 and 1817) and the number of stripes reverted to the original 13, symbolizing the 13 colonies that achieved independence and formed the United States of America. Section 2 of the Act established the principle for future modifications: "And be it further enacted, that on the admission of every new State into the Union, one star be added to the union of the flag; such addition shall take effect on the fourth of July next succeeding such admission." Since then, as more states have joined, there have been some 27 different American flags. The last two states to be admitted were Alaska on January 3, 1959 and Hawaii on August 21, 1959, which means that the last change to the flag was made on July 4, 1960.

For more than 130 years prior to the Flag Act of 1818, there had been no official regulation of the arrangement of the stars in the canton of the national flag. At any given time, the flags displayed dozens of designs, the most popular being concentric rings, ovals, diamonds, and large stars made of smaller stars. Now, however, President Monroe stipulated that the stars should be arranged in parallel rows, an arrangement that was followed by the navy and was officially adopted for all flags in 1912.

It was also in 1912 that the specifications for the construction of the United States flag were laid down—it is sewn in the proportions of 10:19—and those for the colors were written in 1934. National and local laws protect the flag from abuse. Particular stars do not represent particular states—it is simply the total that corresponds to the number of states in the Union. Such is the importance attached to the flag that Uncle Sam, the personification of America, is always dressed in the Stars and Stripes.

The first country to adopt a similar flag to the American one was Hawaii. In an astute political move, the Hawaiian king combined symbols from the flags of the two most influential powers in the Pacific, the British Union Jack with the tricolor stripes of the American ensign, into his nation's flag. Later, other countries—in order to display their solidarity with republican ideals of liberty and democracy—adopted flags that were inspired by the Stars and Stripes. They included Chile (1817), Uruguay (1828), Cuba (1850), and Puerto Rico (1891). Other countries—such as Greece (1822), El Salvador (1865), Brazil (1889), Malaya (1950), and Togo (1960)—have used the stars and/or stripes to represent the number of their states.

State Flags of the USA

Alabama

Adopted on 16 February 1895, the state flag of Alabama bears a red saltire—a crimson cross of St. Andrew —which was the most distinctive feature of the Confederate battle flag.

Alaska

The flag of Alaska was adopted in 1927, following a competition held among the state's school children. It was won by 13-year-old Benny Benson and was chosen for its "simplicity, its originality, and its symbolism." The blue represents the evening sky, the sea, the mountain lakes, and the wild flowers that grow in the state. The golden yellow of the stars symbolize the wealth that is hidden in Alaska's hills and streams, while the pattern of stars reflects the Great Bear—the most conspicuous constellation in the northern sky. The eighth, and largest, star is the North Star (Polaris), by which mariners, explorers, hunters, and prospectors have always determined direction.

Arizona

The red and yellow in the Arizonan flag echo the colors of Spain, reminding us that the first whites to enter the state were Spanish conquistadores in 1540. The copper-colored, five-pointed star in the center of the flag represents the copper mining, the most important industry in Arizona.

Arkansas

The state flag of Arkansas is loaded with symbolism. To start, the colors are those of both the United States national flag and the Confederate States of America. The diamond shape indicates that Arkansas is the only diamond bearing state in the Union, while the 25 stars within its blue border represent the fact that Arkansas was the 25th state admitted to the Union. The star above the name Arkansas commemorates the Confederacy, while the other blue stars represent both Spain, France, and the United States (to which the state has belonged at one time) and the fact that Arkansas was the third state formed out of the Louisiana Purchase.

California

The state flag of California is based on the flag raised in Sonoma on June 14, 1846, when an independent Californian state was proclaimed. Adopted in 1911, the main design device, a grizzly bear, is a symbol of strength, while a red star denotes sovereignty and the white background symbolizes purity.

Colorado

The symbolism of the flag of Colorado is all in the colors. It uses blue (for the sky), yellow (gold reserves), white (snow-capped mountains), and red (the earth). The capital "C" in the center stands for the first letter of the state.

Connecticut

The state flag of Connecticut is based on the design of military colors granted in 1711, during the Civil War. The three grapevines symbolize the state's first three settlements, Hartford, Windsor, and Wethersfield, which formed the colony of Connecticut in 1639.

Delaware

Delaware is known as the "Diamond State," hence the use of a diamond shape in the state flag, and its main industry is agriculture, a fact that is reflected in the arms that are placed in the center of the diamond. The river and boat in the arms also echo the fact that Delaware has access to the sea. The date on the state flag marks the day that Delaware became the first state to ratify the Federal Constitution.

Florida

The state flag of Florida carries a red saltire, similar to those used on Confederate battle flags. The seal at its center depicts a typical Florida scene and includes an American Indian woman out of respect for the original inhabitants of the peninsula.

Georgia

The Georgian flag, which is one of the latest state flags to have been adopted (in 1956), displays both the battle flag of the Confederacy and the state seal, to which are attached the principles of wisdom, justice, and moderation.

Hawaii

This state flag is the same flag that has been used by the Kingdom of Hawaii, the Republic of Hawaii, and the territory of Hawaii ever since 1816. It combines a Union Jack canton with red, white, and blue stripes in the field, similar to those used on American ensigns in the 19th century. Each of the eight stripes represents one of the eight main islands of Hawaii.

Idaho

The state flag of Idaho combines a simple blue field with a coat of arms at its center. In the arms, the woman on the left represents women's suffrage, liberty, and justice, while the miner on the right is an obvious symbol of the state's main industry. The

tree, meanwhile, stands for the state's timber interests, the ploughman and grain represent agriculture, the cornucopias symbolize horticulture, and the elk's head is a reference to the state game laws.

Illinois

On the Illinois state flag, the bald eagle perched on an American shield indicates the state's allegiance to the Union, while the water represents Lake Michigan.

Indiana

The state flag of Indiana is a sea of stars, the largest of which represents Indiana (the 19th state to be admitted to the Union). The other 18 stars symbolize the states that were admitted to the Union prior to Indiana. The torch at the center of the flag stands for liberty and enlightenment, with the rays emanating from it symbolizing their far-reaching effect.

Iowa

The tricolor of Iowa signifies the ties

between the state and France prior to the Louisiana Purchase, while the bald eagle denotes Iowa's current allegiance to the Union.

Kansas

The state flag of Kansas consists of a blue field with an intricate emblem at its center. The sunflower at the top of the emblem is the state flower and the 34 stars in the emblem record the fact that Kansas was the 34th state admitted to the Union. The state's past is represented by a settler's cabin and a train of ox wagons being pursued by native Americans on horseback, while a man ploughing with horses symbolizes the agriculture that has brought prosperity to the state.

Kentucky

This a very simple state flag, bearing an emblem on which two people are embracing, exemplifying the state motto "United we stand, divided we fall." At the bottom of the emblem are two crossed branches of golden rod, the state flower.

Louisiana

The pelican nourishing its young on the state flag of Louisiana signifies self-sacrifice. Underneath, the state motto declares "Union, Justice and Confidence."

Maine

Maine is known as the "Pine Tree State," so it's no surprise that the arms on the state flag feature a white pine. The moose, which is native to Maine, represents the state's large areas of unpolluted forests, while the water symbolizes the sea. There's a farmer to symbolize the land and agriculture, and a sailor to represent the sea and fisheries. Just as on the Alaskan state flag, there's also a North Star, a guiding light for sailors, trappers, and settlers in days gone by.

Maryland

First flown in 1888, the Maryland state flag was not officially adopted until 1904. It is unique among American state flags in that it is an armorial banner, based on the coats of arms of the

Calvert and Crossland families from England. The former was granted to Sir George Calvert, whose sons founded Maryland in 1634, while the latter is that of their grandmother's family.

Massachusetts

The native American holding a bow and arrow on the Massachusetts flag is an old emblem of that part of America, dating back to the early 17th century. The star represents the Commonwealth of Massachusetts and there is a crest of an arm with a sword. The motto "By the sword we seek peace, but peace only under liberty" is a message to the English dating to the years just prior to the Declaration of Independence.

Michigan

This state flag dates to 1837, when it was first used by the Michigan militia, but it was not adopted by the state itself until 1911. Like Illinois and Iowa, it bears a bald eagle, but there is also an elk and a moose, which represent the local fauna. The shield in the cen-

ter of the emblem pays great attention to Michigan's frontier position, with the word "Tuebor" meaning "I will defend" and a man with an upraised right hand symbolizing peace but his left hand on a rifle, indicating his readiness to defend the state.

Minnesota

The 19 stars on this state flag indicate that Minnesota was the 19th state to be admitted to the Union, while the motto "L'Etoile du Nord" (North Star) is a reference to the fact that Minnesota was once the northernmost state of the Union. In the central emblem, a native American is shown giving way to a white settler.

Mississippi

Very patriotic, displaying the colors of the national flag, the state flag of Mississippi also pays homage to the battle flag of the Confederate states in a big way.

Missouri

This is another state flag that uses the

number of stars to recognize the place of the state's admission to the Union—in this case, there are 24. While bears indicate the size and strength of the state, the national arms symbolize the allegiance of Missouri to the Union.

Montana

Although Montana's state flag was officially introduced on July 1, 1981 (on account of the word "Montana" being added to it), the basic design actually dates to 1905 when it was used as the banner of the First Montana Infantry. An emblem in the center of a blue field displays the Great Falls of Missouri and the Rocky Mountains, as well as a plough, shovel, and pick that indicate the state's reliance on agriculture and mining.

Nebraska

Similar in content to that of Montana, as both the Missouri River and Rocky Mountains feature, the state flag of Nebraska also carries a smith representing the state's mechanical arts and grain standing for agriculture. A steamboat and train represent the role of transport.

Nevada

Having been adopted in 1991, Nevada's is the newest state flag. A simple badge in the upper hoist bears a star symbolizing the state, which is white representing silver (Nevada's main mineral)—it is flanked by the state flower, sagebrush. The state motto "Battle Born" is a reminder that Nevada joined the Union during the Civil War.

New Hampshire

An emblem bearing a picture of the frigate *Raleigh*, one of the first 13 vessels ordered by the American navy, is at the center of the blue field of the state flag of New Hampshire. *Raleigh* was built in the New Hampshire port of Portsmouth in 1776.

New Jersey

Unlike many of the other states' blue field, that of New Jersey is "buff"—the regimental color of the New Jersey Continental Line prescribed by George Washington in 1779. The emblem at the center of the flag includes a shield with three ploughs (indicating that New Jersey was the third state admitted to the Union), the figures of Liberty and Ceres (the goddess of agriculture), and a horse's head representing vigor.

New Mexico

The very simple state flag of New Mexico was adopted in 1925. It bears the red and yellow colors of Spain, while the graphic design device at its center is based on the sun symbol used by the ancient Zia Pueblo native Americans who used to inhabit this part of the country.

New York

Parts of the arms at the center of the New York state flag date to the late 18th century and feature the Hudson River, a rising sun symbolizing a bright future, and figures of Liberty and Justice.

North Carolina

This state flag bears the national colors of red, white, and blue, as well as a white star and the initials "NC," both of which represent the state.

North Dakota

This state flag has been adopted from the regimental colors of the First North Dakota Infantry, which fought in the Spanish American War and the Philippine Insurrection, with the addition of the name of the state on a scroll below the central emblem.

Ohio

This is the only state flag to differ from the standard rectangle or square of the other state flags. The unusual shape has been used effectively to represent the hills and valleys of Ohio, while the stripes symbolize the roads and waterways of the state, and the white circle with a red center represents the buckeye, the state tree, from which Ohio gained its nickname "the Buckeye State." Of course, the white "O" also suggests the first letter of Ohio.

Oklahoma

Oklahoma's state flag is unusual in having a paler blue field than most of the state flags—it denotes loyalty and devotion. Meanwhile, the central shield stands for protection and the crossed olive branch and pipe of peace symbolize the state's desire for peace.

Oregon

Oregon's flag is one of the few flags in the world, let alone the only one of the American state flags, to have a different obverse and reverse. The obverse has the state name and date of the state's admission to the Union, plus a gold escutcheon showing two ships (the British one departing, the American one arriving), a covered wagon (representing settlers), a wheatsheaf and plough (denoting agriculture), and a pick (standing for mining), while the reverse carries a picture of a golden beaver.

Pennsylvania

This rather grand state flag carries a large emblem with an eagle denoting allegiance to the Union, and a ship, plough, and three wheatsheafs taken from the arms of the counties of Philadelphia, Chester, and Sussex (which were part of Pennsylvania at one point) respectively.

Rhode Island

Rhode Island's state flag has one of the oldest provenances of all the country's state flags: an anchor with the word "Hope" has appeared on seals for the state since 1664. The 13 gold stars around the gold anchor and "Hope" represent the 13 original states of the Union.

South Carolina

While this state flag looks fairly modern, its roots actually date to the 18th century. The crescent reproduces a silver badge (with the inscription "Liberty or Death") that was worn on soldiers' caps in two of the South Carolina regiments who fought during the American Revolution. The palm tree was adopted as a symbol of victory in 1776, when the fort (which was built from palm tree trunks) at Sullivan's Island in Charleston Harbour, defeated the British fleet.

South Dakota

South Dakota, known as "The Mount Rushmore State," was formerly called "The Sunshine State," hence the prominent part played by the sun in the state flag. Inside the sun, the state seal depicts a typical landscape with a ploughman symbolizing agriculture, the steamboat transportation, the smelting furnace the mining industry, the cattle dairy farming, and the trees lumbering.

Tennessee

The patriotically colored Tennessee state flag has three white stars, which denote the three geographical divisions of the state and the fact that Tennessee was the third state to be admitted into the Union after the original 13. Set on blue, with a white circle surround symbolizing unity, the main field of the flag is red.

Texas

Originally known as The Lone Star Flag, it was designed for the Republic of Texas and became the state flag when Texas joined the Union in 1845. The red, white, and blue colors stand for bravery, purity, and loyalty respectively.

Utah

At the center of the emblem of the Utah state flag are a beehive, representing industry (the main virtue of the original settlers), and sego lilies, which are a symbol of peace. Both the eagle and the caricatures of the Stars and Stripes indicate the state's support for the Union.

Vermont

Adopted in 1923, the elegant Vermont state flag carries a pine tree, the traditional emblem of New England, sheaves of wheat and a cow, both of which represent agriculture.

Virginia

On the Virginia state flag stands Virtus, the symbol of the Commonwealth, dressed as an Amazon with her foot squarely on Tyranny, which is represented by the prostrate body of a man holding a broken chain and scourge in his hands. The message is clear: "Thus Ever To Tyrants."

Washington

The field of Washington's flag is green, —the state's nickname is "The Evergreen State." In its center there is a picture of George Washington that was adopted in 1967, instead of the seal that had been used since 1889, when Washington became a state of the Union.

West Virginia

The main color of this state flag is white, representing the purity of state institutions; the blue of the border stands for the Union. The main features of the emblem are a farmer and miner, symbolizing West Virginia's two main industries.

Wisconsin

Although this state flag was adopted in 1913, the word "Wisconsin" and the date "1848" were not added until 1981. In the middle of the blue field is a coat of arms displaying symbols of agriculture, mining, manufacture, and navigation; flanking it either side are a sailor and a miner, who represent labor on water and land respectively. Above the arms is a badger, referring to Wisconsin's nickname of "The Badger State."

Wyoming

The main feature of this state flag is a bison, which represents Wyoming's local fauna. Other important characteristics are the red border, standing for the native Americans and the blood of the pioneers; the white inner border that is a symbol of purity and morality; and the expanse of blue denoting the skies and distant mountains, as well as being a symbol of fidelity, justice, and virility.

District of Columbia

The DC state flag is taken straight from the Washington family coat of arms.

The Dutch and pan-Slav Colors

The Dutch "Prinsenvlag," with its orange, blue, and white horizontal stripes, was created around 1600 from the flags under which the Netherlands fought for independence from Spain in the 16th century. It played a key role in flag history, because it was the first "modern" flag to display simple stripes, rather than heraldic devices. Orange was chosen to commemorate the Dutch leader, William I, Prince of Orange (1533–84), while blue and white were Christian colors. William's soldiers originally wore armbands in these colors at the siege of Leiden in 1574. Then, in the 1580s, the colors were transferred onto flags used on land and the horizontal tricolor of ensigns.

The Dutch flag—the world's first "modern" flag.

During the 17th century, the orange was gradually replaced by red. There are two possible reasons for this change: it may have been because red is more visible at sea or because political opponents wanted to exclude the House of Orange. Whatever the real reason, the original tricolor survived only until around 1795, when the orange was officially replaced by red.

In the 18th century, the Dutch ensign became well known in many parts of the world, especially South East Asia, North America, and South Africa, and thus became the inspiration for a great number of flags. In South Africa, for example, seven political entities adopted flags based on the Dutch design: Natalia (1839), Transvaal (1857), Orange Free State (1857), Lyndenburg Republic (1857), Goshen Republic (1882), New Republic (1884), and the Union of South Africa (1928). In America, the original Dutch colors appear on the flag of New York (formerly known as New Amsterdam), which is widely used in the city to this day, while the modern colors (including red rather than orange) appear on the flag of the Netherlands Antilles.

By a strange quirk of fate, the Dutch flag has had an even greater impact on the flags of Slav nations. In 1697, Tsar Peter the Great (1672–1725), who was keen to modernize his country, travelled incognito to western Europe to learn all about advancing technologies, particularly those relating to the shipbuilding industry. He worked for four months in the shipyard of the Dutch East India Company in Zaandam and also spent time in the British Navy shipyard at Deptford. Returning to Russia, he then introduced an elaborate system of naval flags based on Dutch and British flags and ensigns, including the country's first merchant flag, which he designed himself in 1699 based on the Prinsenvlag. This flag, a horizontal tricolor of white, blue, and red, would go on to become the national flag of Russia.

And this flag, in turn, inspired other Slav countries to adopt horizontal tricolors that used the same colors in different arrangements. In 1835, the Serbs adopted a red, blue, and white tricolor for their ships to use on inland waters. Thirteen years later, during the first pan-Slav Congress in Prague, the very same colors were proclaimed as pan-Slav colors and horizontal tricolors were subsequently adopted by several Slav provinces of Austria. The Slovaks and Slovenes placed the colors in the same order as Russia, while the Serbs adopted a blue, red, and white tricolor, and the Croats positioned the colors in the same way as the Dutch flag. The flag adopted by Bulgaria in 1878 was the same as that of Russia, but it used green instead of red. In 1880, Montenegro adopted a tricolor as its merchant ensign that was similar to that of Serbia—one difference was that it had a white cross in the center of the red stripe. The Kingdom of Serbs, Croats, and Slovenes, which was established in 1918, adopted a national flag and ensign in the form of a horizontal blue, white, and red tricolor, which remains in use today by the same country, now known as Yugoslavia.

Other flags that do not belong to this family, but were still inspired by it because their design (a horizontal tricolor) was copied from that of the Russian flag include a number of countries that were once part of the Russian Empire, for example Lithuania (1918) and Estonia (1881).

The French Tricolore

Some of the best known flags in history have been French. The first was the "Oriflamme," a scarlet flag with an unusual, many-tailed shape that was adopted as the banner of the French in the Middle Ages. The second is the "Tricolore."

The colors red, blue, and white have been used on French flags since the time of Charlemagne in the eighth century. Charlemagne adopted red as the color of the imperial flag; both the armorial banner of France and the merchant ensign from 1661 to 1790 had a blue field from the 13th century to 1589; and white was the color of the French flag and ensign from 1589 to 1790. However, it has more to do with coincidence than history that all these three colors appear together on the French national flag, which was created from the red and blue of the Parisian coat of arms, and the white of the Bourbons.

During the French Revolution, the Paris militia wore blue and red cockades (ribbons that were worn on military headgear) and, when the monarchy was deposed, one was presented to King Louis XVI, who attached it to his royal white one. The leaders of the Revolution immediately decided to adopt this new cockade in the "colors of liberty." Enthusiastically received by the people, the streets of Paris were soon awash with ribbons and flags in the "colors of liberty." A year later, a new ensign was adopted that was white with a canton composed of a red, white, and blue vertical tricolor; a white border separated it from the outer border, which was half-red and half-blue. The vertical arrangement of three colors was revolutionary, both vexillologically and politically speaking. On February 15, 1794, the order of colors in the French tricolor was changed to the present one.

A few decades after the French Revolution, the colors of the French flag came to be perceived in Europe and elsewhere as the colors of the republican movement and were adopted by

The colors of the French flag have been adopted by countries around the world.

countries as far-flung as Uruguay (1825–28), the Dominican Republic (1844), and Costa Rica (1848). Even more influential was the 'Tricolore' design that Napoleon introduced to some Italian states—it inspired revolutionaries and leaders of independence movements in many parts of the world to adopt flags with a vertical arrangement of colors. For example, revolutionary movements or governments in Mexico (1815), Belgium (1831), Colombia (1834), Ecuador (1845), Ireland (1848), Italy (1848), and Iraq (1958) all adopted flags with three vertical stripes.

Other flags in the French family include those belonging to former French colonies in Africa, for example Senegal and Mali, which adopted flags following the "Tricolore" design when they gained independence in the second half of the 20th century.

Some other important flags that do not form part of the tricolor family but originated in France are the red flag and the anarchist flag. The red flag dates to the French Revolution, but was also used in the Paris Commune (1870) and the Russian Revolution of 1905. However, it was not until the success of the 1917 Bolshevik Revolution that it became the flag of Russia, and then the Soviet Union (1924). It was subsequently copied by communist regimes in Vietnam, China, and Africa. And, even though many communist regimes have now been supplanted, the Red Flag remains the flag of the extreme left and is widely used in one form or another as a left-wing party flag. The anarchist flag, which was also first used during the French Revolution, is a variant of the red flag. The addition of black denotes "Liberty or Death" and, in this form, was used in Haiti (1810). It also influenced the German Tricolor of 1818, and gave rise to the flags of Angola and Cuba's Fidel Castro; to this day, the Sandinista rebels in Nicaragua use it.

The Livery Colors

The simplest national flags belong to the livery family. In other words, they are the flags introduced by several European countries in the last 200 years or so that are composed of livery colors arranged in two or three horizontal stripes. Usually, the upper stripe is the color of a heraldic charge, while the lower stripe displays the color of the shield, although the reverse order is typical of Austria. Almost always, when translating coats of arms into flags, gold becomes yellow and silver becomes white. The exception to the rule is obvious in the German flag, which bears a golden yellow stripe along with red and black.

Livery flags have always been popular on the Iberian peninsula. The Spanish national flag is a good example: yellow and red are the armorial colors of Castile, Aragon, Catalonia, and Navarre. And during the Spanish republic (1931–39), the colors used on the flag were red, yellow, and purple, which are the colors of the lion in the arms of Leon. Between 1821 and 1910, the Portuguese flag displayed livery colors dating from the 12th century. Today, other national flags using livery colors include those of San Marino, Luxembourg, Monaco, the Vatican, Poland, and Ukraine.

Victorious Spanish soccer players celebrate with the national flag.

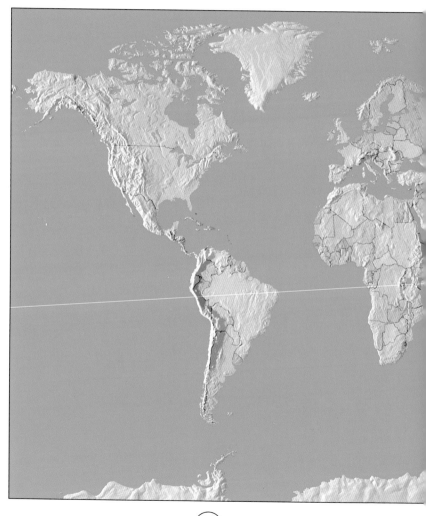

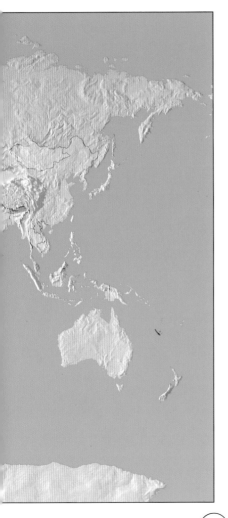

PART TWO

GAZETTEER

UNITED NATIONS

Member States— (Date of Admission)

Afghanistan—(19 Nov. 1946)
Albania—(14 Dec. 1955)
Algeria—(8 Oct. 1962)
Andorra—(28 July 1993)
Angola—(1 Dec. 1976)
Antigua and Barbuda—
  (11 Nov. 1981)
Argentina—(24 Oct. 1945)
Armenia—(2 Mar. 1992)
Australia—(1 Nov. 1945)
Austria—(14 Dec. 1955)
Azerbaijan—(9 Mar. 1992)

Bahamas—(18 Sep. 1973)
Bahrain—(21 Sep. 1971)
Bangladesh—(17 Sep. 1974)
Barbados—(9 Dec. 1966)
Belarus—(24 Oct. 1945)
Belgium—(27 Dec. 1945)
Belize—(25 Sep. 1981)
Benin—(20 Sep. 1960)
Bhutan—(21 Sep. 1971)
Bolivia—(14 Nov. 1945)
Bosnia and Herzegovina—
  (22 May 1992)
Botswana—(17 Oct. 1966)

Brazil—(24 Oct. 1945)
Brunei Darussalam—
  (21 Sep. 1984)
Bulgaria—(14 Dec. 1955)
Burkina Faso—(20 Sep. 1960)
Burundi—(18 Sep. 1962)

Cambodia—(14 Dec. 1955)
Cameroon—(20 Sep. 1960)
Canada—(9 Nov. 1945)
Cape Verde—(16 Sep. 1975)
Central African Republic—
  (20 Sep. 1960)
Chad—(20 Sep. 1960)
Chile—(24 Oct. 1945)
China—(24 Oct. 1945)
Colombia—(5 Nov. 1945)
Comoros—(12 Nov. 1975)
Congo—(20 Sep. 1960)
Costa Rica—(2 Nov. 1945)
Côte d'Ivoire—(20 Sep. 1960)
Croatia—(22 May 1992)
Cuba—(24 Oct. 1945)
Cyprus—(20 Sep. 1960)
Czech Republic—
  (19 Jan. 1993)

Democratic People's Republic
  of Korea—(17 Sep. 1991)
Democratic Republic of the
  Congo—(20 Sep. 1960)
Denmark—(24 Oct. 1945)
Djibouti—(20 Sep. 1977)
Dominica—(18 Dec. 1978)
Dominican Republic—
  (24 Oct. 1945)

Ecuador—(21 Dec. 1945)
Egypt—(24 Oct. 1945)
El Salvador—(24 Oct. 1945)
Equatorial Guinea—
  (12 Nov. 1968)
Eritrea—(28 May 1993)

Estonia—(17 Sep. 1991)
Ethiopia—(13 Nov. 1945)

Fiji—(13 Oct. 1970)
Finland—(14 Dec. 1955)
France—(24 Oct. 1945)

Gabon—(20 Sep. 1960)
Gambia—(21 Sep. 1965)
Georgia—(31 July 1992)
Germany—(18 Sep. 1973)
Ghana—(8 Mar. 1957)
Greece—(25 Oct. 1945)
Grenada—(17 Sep. 1974)
Guatemala—(21 Nov. 1945)
Guinea—(12 Dec. 1958)
Guinea-Bissau—(17 Sep. 1974)
Guyana—(20 Sep. 1966)

Haiti—(24 Oct. 1945)
Honduras—(17 Dec. 1945)
Hungary—(14 Dec. 1955)

Iceland—(19 Nov. 1946)
India—(30 Oct. 1945)
Indonesia—(28 Sep. 1950)
Iran (Islamic Republic of)—
  (24 Oct. 1945)
Iraq—(21 Dec. 1945)
Ireland—(14 Dec. 1955)
Israel—(11 May 1949)
Italy—(14 Dec. 1955)
Jamaica—(18 Sep. 1962)

Japan—(18 Dec. 1956)
Jordan—(14 Dec. 1955)

Kazakhstan—(2 Mar. 1992)
Kenya—(16 Dec. 1963)
Kiribati—(14 Sept. 1999)
Kuwait—(14 May 1963)
Kyrgyzstan—(2 Mar. 1992)

Lao People's Democratic
    Republic—(14 Dec. 1955)
Latvia—(17 Sep. 1991)
Lebanon—(24 Oct. 1945)
Lesotho—(17 Oct. 1966)
Liberia—(2 Nov. 1945)
Libyan Arab Jamahiriya—
    (14 Dec. 1955)
Liechtenstein—(18 Sep. 1990)
Lithuania—(17 Sep. 1991)
Luxembourg—(24 Oct. 1945)

Madagascar—(20 Sep. 1960)
Malawi—(1 Dec. 1964)
Malaysia—(17 Sep. 1957)
Maldives—(21 Sep. 1965)
Mali—(28 Sep. 1960)
Malta—(1 Dec. 1964)
Marshall Islands—
    (17 Sep. 1991)
Mauritania—(7 Oct. 1961)
Mauritius—(24 Apr. 1968)
Mexico—(7 Nov. 1945)
Micronesia (Federated States
    of)—(17 Sep. 1991)
Monaco—(28 May 1993)
Mongolia—(27 Oct. 1961)
Morocco—(12 Nov. 1956)
Mozambique—(16 Sep. 1975)
Myanmar—(19 Apr. 1948)

Namibia—(23 Apr. 1990)
Nauru—(14 Sept. 1999)
Nepal—(14 Dec. 1955)
Netherlands—(10 Dec. 1945)
New Zealand—(24 Oct. 1945)
Nicaragua—(24 Oct. 1945)
Niger—(20 Sep. 1960)
Nigeria—(7 Oct. 1960)
Norway—(27 Nov. 1945)

Oman—(7 Oct. 1971)

Pakistan—(30 Sep. 1947)
Palau—(15 Dec. 1994)
Panama—(13 Nov. 1945)
Papua New Guinea—
    (10 Oct. 1975)
Paraguay—(24 Oct. 1945)
Peru—(31 Oct. 1945)
Philippines—(24 Oct. 1945)
Poland—(24 Oct. 1945)
Portugal—(14 Dec. 1955)

Qatar—(21 Sep. 1971)

Republic of Korea—
    (17 Sep. 1991)
Republic of Moldova—
    (2 Mar. 1992)
Romania—(14 Dec. 1955)
Russian Federation—
    (24 Oct. 1945)
Rwanda—(18 Sep. 1962)

Saint Kitts and Nevis—
    (23 Sep. 1983)
Saint Lucia—(18 Sep. 1979)
Saint Vincent and the
    Grenadines—
    (16 Sep. 1980)
Samoa—(15 Dec. 1976)
San Marino—(2 Mar. 1992)
Sao Tome and Principe—
    (16 Sep. 1975)
Saudi Arabia—(24 Oct. 1945)
Senegal—(28 Sep. 1960)
Seychelles—(21 Sep. 1976)
Sierra Leone—(27 Sep. 1961)
Singapore—(21 Sep. 1965)
Slovakia—(19 Jan. 1993)
Slovenia—(22 May 1992)
Solomon Islands—
    (19 Sep. 1978)
Somalia—(20 Sep. 1960)
South Africa—(7 Nov. 1945)

Spain—(14 Dec. 1955)
Sri Lanka—(14 Dec. 1955)
Sudan—(12 Nov. 1956)
Suriname—(4 Dec. 1975)
Swaziland—(24 Sep. 1968)
Sweden—(19 Nov. 1946)
Syrian Arab Republic—
    (24 Oct. 1945)

Tajikistan—(2 Mar. 1992)
Thailand—(16 Dec. 1946)
Togo—(20 Sep. 1960)
Tonga—(14 Sept. 1999)
Trinidad and Tobago—
    (18 Sep. 1962)
Tunisia—(12 Nov. 1956)
Turkey—(24 Oct. 1945)
Turkmenistan—(2 Mar. 1992)
Tuvalu—(5 Sept. 2000)

Uganda—(25 Oct. 1962)
Ukraine—(24 Oct. 1945)
United Arab Emirates—
    (9 Dec. 1971)
United Kingdom of Great
    Britain and Northern
    Ireland—(24 Oct. 1945)
United Republic of Tanzania—
    (14 Dec. 1961)
United States of America—
    (24 Oct. 1945)
Uruguay—(18 Dec. 1945)
Uzbekistan—(2 Mar. 1992)

Vanuatu—(15 Sep. 1981)
Venezuela—(15 Nov. 1945)
Viet Nam—(20 Sep. 1977)

Yemen—(30 Sep. 1947)
Yugoslavia—(1 Nov. 2000)

Zambia—(1 Dec. 1964)
Zimbabwe—(25 Aug. 1980)

AFRICA

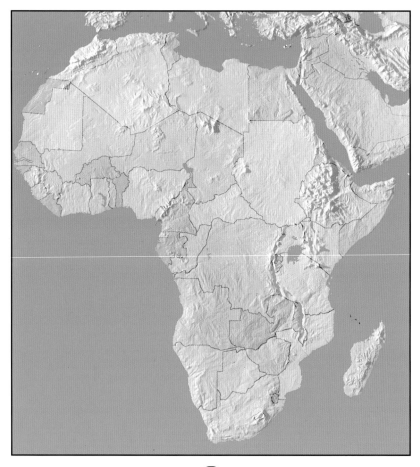

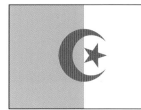

ALGERIA

Capital: El Djezair (Algiers)
Area (sq km): 2,381,745
Population: 31,193,917 (July 2000 est)
Languages: Arabic, Berber, French
Principal religions: Muslim
Currency: Algerian dinar
GDP per capita (in US$): 1,097
Adult illiteracy percentage: 36.7%
Life expectancy (male/female):
  67.5/70.3

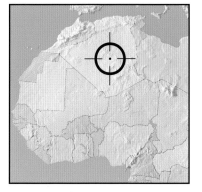

ANGOLA

Capital: Luanda
Area (sq km): 1,246,700
Population: 10,145,267 (July 2000 est)
Languages: Portuguese, Bantu
Principal religions: Christian,
  Animist
Currency: Kwanza
GDP per capita (in US$): 663
Adult illiteracy percentage: 58%
Life expectancy (male/female):
  37.11/39.56

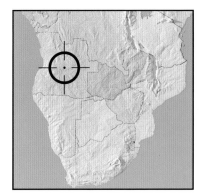

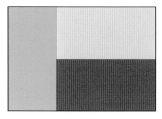

BENIN

Capital: Porto Novo
Area (sq km): 112,620
Population: 6,395,919 (July 2000 est)
Languages: French, Fon, Yoruba
Principal religions: indigenous,
    Christian, Muslim
Currency: CFA franc
GDP per capita (in US$): 364
Adult illiteracy percentage: 62.5%
Life expectancy (male/female):
    49.24/51.16

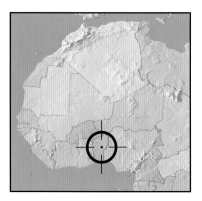

BOTSWANA

Capital: Gaberone
Area (sq km): 575,000
Population: 1,576,470 (July 2000 est)
Languages: Setswana, English
Principal religions: indigenous,
    Christian
Currency: Pula
GDP per capita (in US$): 3,209
Adult illiteracy percentage: 22.8%
Life expectancy (male/female):
    38.63/39.93

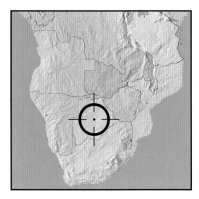

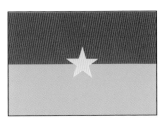

BURKINA FASO

Capital: Ouagadougou
Area (sq km): 274,122
Population: 11,946,065 (July 2000 est)
Languages: French, local languages
Principal religions: indigenous,
Muslim
Currency: CFA franc
GDP per capita (in US$): 160
Adult illiteracy percentage: 77%
Life expectancy (male/female):
46.29/47.18

BURUNDI

Capital: Bujumbura
Area (sq km): 27,835
Population: 6,054,714 (July 2000 est)
Languages: French, Kirundi, Kiswahili
Principal religions: Roman
Catholic, Muslim
Currency: Burundi franc
GDP per capita (in US$): 126
Adult illiteracy percentage: 51.9%
Life expectancy (male/female):
45.23/47.16

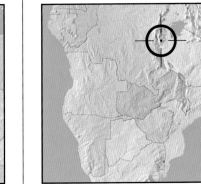

CAMEROON

Capital: Yaounde
Area (sq km): 475,000
Population: 15,421,937 (July 2000 est)
Languages: French, English,
indigenous languages
Principal religions: indigenous,
Christian, Muslim
Currency: CFA franc
GDP per capita (in US$): 617
Adult illiteracy percentage: 24.6%
Life expectancy (male/female):
54.01/55.64

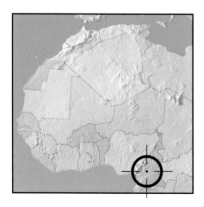

CAPE VERDE

Capital: Praia
Area (sq km): 4,035
Population: 401,343 (July 2000 est)
Languages: Portuguese, Creole
Principal religions: Roman
Catholic, Protestant
Currency: Escudo Caboverdiano
GDP per capita (in US$): 833
Adult illiteracy percentage: 26.5%
Life expectancy (male/female):
65.63/72.29

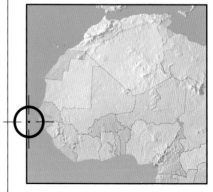

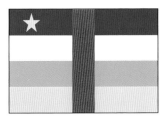

CENTRAL AFRICAN REPUBLIC

Capital: Bangui
Area (sq km): 624,975
Population: 3,512,751 (July 2000 est)
Languages: French, Sango,
indigenous languages
Principal religions: Protestant,
Roman Catholic, Muslim,
indigenous
Currency: CFA franc
GDP per capita (in US$): 364
Adult illiteracy percentage: 53.5%
Life expectancy (male/female):
42.26/45.84

CHAD

Capital: Ndjamena
Area (sq km): 1,284,000
Population: 8,424,504 (July 2000 est)
Languages: French, Arabic
Principal religions: Muslim,
Christian, indigenous
Currency: CFA franc
GDP per capita (in US$): 149
Adult illiteracy percentage: 46.4%
Life expectancy (male/female):
48.5/52.56

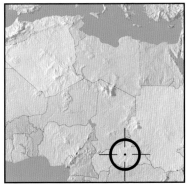

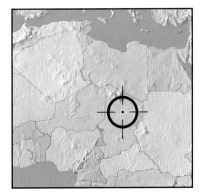

COMOROS

Capital: Moroni
Area (sq km): 1,860
Population: 578,400 (July 2000 est)
Languages: French, Arabic
Principal religions: Muslim
Currency: Cormoran franc
GDP per capita (in US$): 334
Adult illiteracy percentage: 43.8%
Life expectancy (male/female):
  57.85/62.28

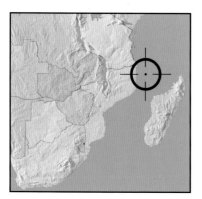

CONGO

Capital: Brazzaville
Area (sq km): 342,000
Population: 2,830,961 (July 2000 est)
Languages: French, indigenous
  languages
Principal religions: Roman
  Catholic, indigenous
Currency: CFA franc
GDP per capita (in US$): 702
Adult illiteracy percentage: 19.3%
Life expectancy (male/female):
  44.49/50.47

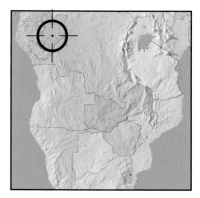

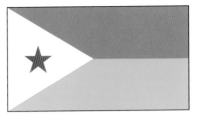

IVORY COAST

Capital: Yamoussoukro (official);
Abidjan (de facto)
Area (sq km): 322,465
Population: 15,980,950 (July 2000 est)
Languages: French, local languages
Principal religions: Muslim, Roman
Catholic, indigenous
Currency: CFA franc
GDP per capita (in US$): 731
Adult illiteracy percentage: 53.2%
Life expectancy (male/female):
43.72/46.63

DJIBOUTI

Capital: Djibouti
Area (sq km): 23,000
Population: 451,442 (July 2000 est)
Languages: Arabic, French, Afar,
Somali
Principal religions: Muslim, Roman
Catholic
Currency: Djibouti franc
GDP per capita (in US$): 979
Adult illiteracy percentage: 48.6%
Life expectancy (male/female):
49.01/52.68

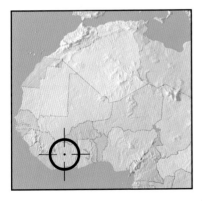

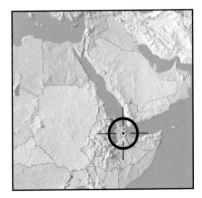

EGYPT

Capital: Cairo
Area (sq km): 1,000,250
Population: 68,359,979 (July 2000 est)
Languages: Arabic, French, English, Berber
Principal religions: Sunni Muslim, Christian
Currency: Egyptian pound
GDP per capita (in US$): 1,168
Adult illiteracy percentage: 44.7%
Life expectancy (male/female): 61.29/65.47

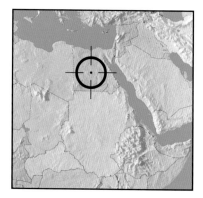

EQUATORIAL GUINEA

Capital: Malabo
Area (sq km): 28,050
Population: 474,214 (July 2000 est)
Languages: Spanish, Fang, Bantu
Principal religions: Roman Catholic
Currency: CFA franc
GDP per capita (in US$): 349
Adult illiteracy percentage: 16.8%
Life expectancy (male/female): 51.53/55.65

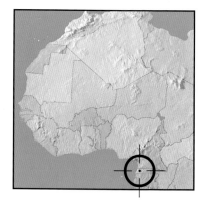

ERITREA

Capital: Asmara
Area (sq km): 91,600
Population: 4,135,933 (July 2000 est)
Languages: Tigrinya, Tigre, Arabic, English
Principal religions: Muslim, Ethiopian Orthodox
Currency: Nakfa
GDP per capita (in US$): 173
Adult illiteracy percentage: (Data not available)
Life expectancy (male/female): 52.36/58.29

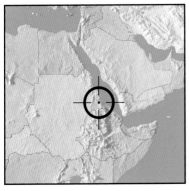

ETHIOPIA

Capital: Addis Adaba
Area (sq km): 1,104,300
Population: 64,117,452 (July 2000 est)
Languages: Amharic, Galla, Tigrinya
Principal religions: Muslim, Christian, indigenous
Currency: Ethiopean birr
GDP per capita (in US$): 186 (1991)
Adult illiteracy percentage: 61.3%
Life expectancy (male/female): 44.41/45.94

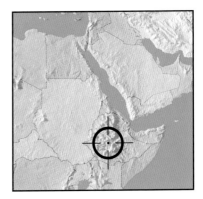

GABON

Capital: Libreville
Area (sq km): 267,665
Population: 1,208,436 (July 2000 est)
Languages: French, Bantu
Principal religions: Roman
Catholic, indigenous
Currency: CFA franc
GDP per capita (in US$): 4,611
Adult illiteracy percentage: 29.2%
Life expectancy (male/female):
48.94/51.26

THE GAMBIA

Capital: Banjul
Area (sq km): 10,690
Population: 1,367,124 (July 2000 est)
Languages: English, Mandinka, Wolof
Principal religions: Muslim,
Christian
Currency: Dalasi
GDP per capita (in US$): 323
Adult illiteracy percentage: 63.5%
Life expectancy (male/female):
51.29/55.16

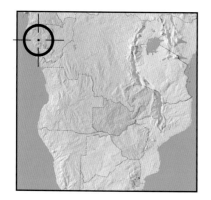

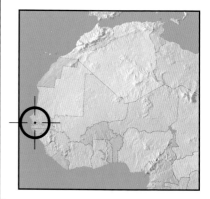

GHANA

Capital: Accra
Area (sq km): 238,305
Population: 19,533,560 (July 2000 est)
Languages: English, French, Akan,
Mossi, Ewe, Ga-Adangme
Principal religions: Animist,
Christian, Muslim, indigenous
Currency: Cedi
GDP per capita (in US$): 398
Adult illiteracy percentage: 29.8%
Life expectancy (male/female):
56.07/58.82

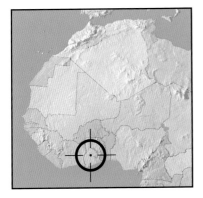

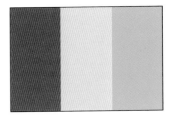

GUINEA

Capital: Conakry
Area (sq km): 245,855
Population: 7,466,200 (July 2000 est)
Languages: French, Susu, Fulani,
Malinke
Principal religions: Muslim,
indigenous
Currency: Guinean franc
GDP per capita (in US$): 535
Adult illiteracy percentage: 58.9%
Life expectancy (male/female):
46/47

GUINEA-BISSAU

Capital: Bissau
Area (sq km): 36,125
Population: 1,285,715 (July 2000 est)
Languages: Portuguese, Creole, local languages
Principal religions: indigenous, Muslim
Currency: Peso
GDP per capita (in US$): 96
Adult illiteracy percentage: 63.2%
Life expectancy (male/female): 46.77/51.37

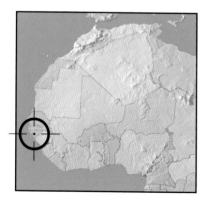

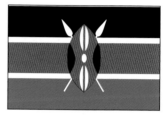

KENYA

Capital: Nairobi
Area (sq km): 582,645
Population: 30,339,770 (July 2000 est)
Languages: Swahili, Kikuyu, Luo, English
Principal religions: Christian, Muslim, indigenous
Currency: Kenya shilling
GDP per capita (in US$): 356
Adult illiteracy percentage: 17.5%
Life expectancy (male/female): 46.95/49.04

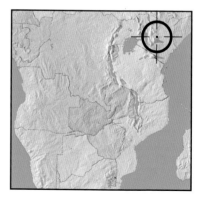

LESOTHO

Capital: Maseru
Area (sq km): 30,345
Population: 2,143,141 (July 2000 est)
Languages: Sesotho, English
Principal religions: Christian
Currency: Loti
GDP per capita (in US$): 505
Adult illiteracy percentage: 16.1%
Life expectancy (male/female):
49.78/51.84

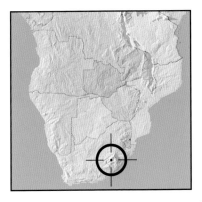

LIBERIA

Capital: Monrovia
Area (sq km): 111,370
Population: 3,164,156 (July 2000 est)
Languages: English, Mande, West
Atlantic, Kwa
Principal religions: Muslim,
Christian, indigenous
Currency: Liberian dollar
GDP per capita (in US$): 1,242
Adult illiteracy percentage: 46.6%
Life expectancy (male/female):
49.6/52.49

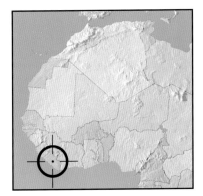

LIBYAN ARAB JAMAHIRIYA

Capital: Tarabulus (Tripoli)
Area (sq km): 1,759,540
Population: 5,115,450 (July 2000 est)
Languages: Arabic, Berber
Principal religions: Muslim
Currency: Libyan dinar
GDP per capita (in US$): 5,621
Adult illiteracy percentage: 20.2%
Life expectancy (male/female):
    73.34/77.66

MADAGASCAR

Capital: Antananarivo
Area (sq km): 594,180
Population: 15,506,472 (July 2000 est)
Languages: Malagasy, French, English
Principal religions: indigenous,
    Christian, Muslim
Currency: Malagasy franc
GDP per capita (in US$): 122
Adult illiteracy percentage: 20%
Life expectancy (male/female):
    52.71/57.26

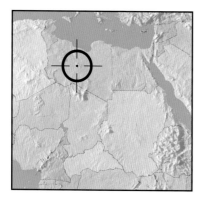

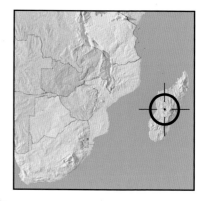

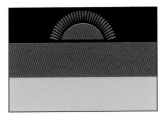

MALAWI

Capital: Lilongwe
Area (sq km): 94,080
Population: 10,385,849 (July 2000 est)
Languages: Chichewa, English, Bantu
Principal religions: Christian,
Muslim
Currency: Kwacha
GDP per capita (in US$): 234
Adult illiteracy percentage: 39.7%
Life expectancy (male/female):
37.2/37.98

MALI

Capital: Bamako
Area (sq km): 1,240,140
Population: 10,685,948 (July 2000 est)
Languages: French, Bambara, Senufo
Principal religions: Muslim, indige-
nous
Currency: CFA franc
GDP per capita (in US$): 244
Adult illiteracy percentage: 59.7%
Life expectancy (male/female):
45.5/47.85

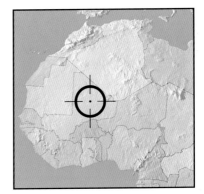

MAURITANIA

Capital: Nouakchott
Area (sq km): 1,030,700
Population: 2,211,000 (July 2000 est)
Languages: Arabic, French, Pular,
Soninke, Wolof
Principal religions: Muslim
Currency: Ouguiya
GDP per capita (in US$): 388
Adult illiteracy percentage: 60.1%
Life expectancy (male/female):
48.7/52.87

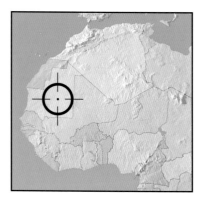

MAURITIUS

Capital: Port Louis
Area (sq km): 1,865
Population: 1,179,368 (July 2000 est)
Languages: English, Creole, Hindi,
French
Principal religions: Hindu,
Christian, Muslim
Currency: Mauritius rupee
GDP per capita (in US$): 3,688
Adult illiteracy percentage: 15.7%
Life expectancy (male/female):
66.98/75.04

MOROCCO

Capital: Rabat
Area (sq km): 710,850
Population: 30,122,350 (July 2000 est)
Languages: Arabic, Berber, French
Principal religions: Sunni Muslim
Currency: Dirham
GDP per capita (in US$): 1,246
Adult illiteracy percentage: 51.1%
Life expectancy (male/female):
66.92/71.44

MOZAMBIQUE

Capital: Maputo
Area (sq km): 784,755
Population: 19,104,696 (July 2000 est)
Languages: Portuguese, Swahili,
Bantu
Principal religions: indigenous,
Christian, Muslim
Currency: Metical
GDP per capita (in US$): 94
Adult illiteracy percentage: 56.2%
Life expectancy (male/female):
38.34/36.68

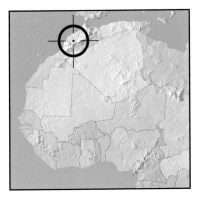

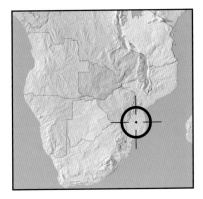

NAMIBIA

Capital: Windhoek
Area (sq km): 824,295
Population: 1,771,327 (July 2000 est)
Languages: English, Afrikaans,
German, indigenous languages
Principal religions: Christian,
Animist
Currency: Namibia dollar and South
African rand
GDP per capita (in US$): 2,046
Adult illiteracy percentage: 17.9%
Life expectancy (male/female):
44.33/40.53

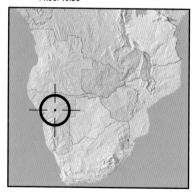

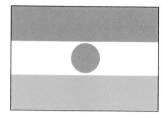

NIGER

Capital: Niamey
Area (sq km): 1,186,410
Population: 10,075,511 (July 2000 est)
Languages: French, Hausa, Djerma
Principal religions: Muslim,
Christian, indigenous
Currency: CFA franc
GDP per capita (in US$): 191
Adult illiteracy percentage: 84.3%
Life expectancy (male/female):
41.43/41.11

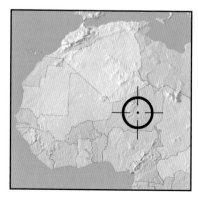

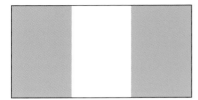

NIGERIA

Capital: Abuja
Area (sq km): 923,850
Population: 123,337,822 (July 2000 est)
Languages: English, Hausa, Ibo, Yoruba
Principal religions: Muslim, Christian, indigenous
Currency: Naira
GDP per capita (in US$): 1,376
Adult illiteracy percentage: 35.9%
Life expectancy (male/female): 51.58/51.55

REUNION

Capital: Saint-Denis
Area (sq km): 2,510
Population: 720,934 (July 2000 est)
Languages: French
Principal religions: Roman Catholic
Currency: French franc
GDP per capita (in US$): 10,767
Adult illiteracy percentage: 12.9%
Life expectancy (male/female): 69.28/76.24

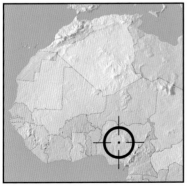

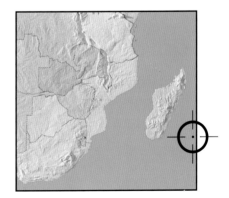

RWANDA

Capital: Kigali
Area (sq km): 26,330
Population: 7,229,129 (July 2000 est)
Languages: Kinyarawanda, French, Kiswahili, Watsui, English
Principal religions: Roman Catholic, Protestant, Muslim, indigenous
Currency: Rwanda franc
GDP per capita (in US$): 170
Adult illiteracy percentage: 33%
Life expectancy (male/female): 38.58/40.13

SAO TOME AND PRINCIPE

Capital: Sao Tome
Area (sq km): 964
Population: 159,883 (July 2000 est)
Languages: Potuguese, Fang
Principal religions: Roman Catholic, Animist
Currency: Dobra
GDP per capita (in US$): 318
Adult illiteracy percentage: 37%
Life expectancy (male/female): 63.84/66.7

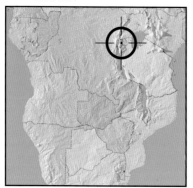

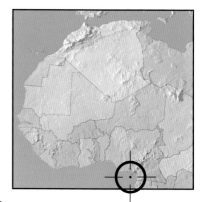

SENEGAL

Capital: Dakar
Area (sq km): 196,720
Population: 9,987,494 (July 2000 est)
Languages: French, Wolof, indigenous languages
Principal religions: Sunni Muslim, Christian, Animist
Currency: CFA franc
GDP per capita (in US$): 519
Adult illiteracy percentage: 62.7%
Life expectancy (male/female): 60.6/63.82

SEYCHELLES

Capital: Victoria
Area (sq km): 404
Population: 79,326 (July 2000 est)
Languages: English, French, Creole
Principal religions: Roman Catholic
Currency: Seychelles rupee
GDP per capita (in US$): 7,304
Adult illiteracy percentage: 11%
Life expectancy (male/female): 64.87/76.12

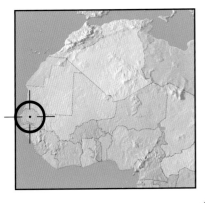

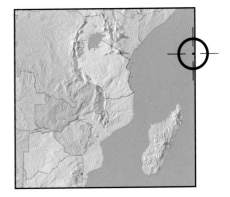

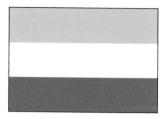

SIERRA LEONE

Capital: Freetown
Area (sq km): 72,325
Population: 5,232,624 (July 2000 est)
Languages: English, Creole
Principal religions: indigenous,
   Muslim, Christian
Currency: Leone
GDP per capita (in US$): 260
Adult illiteracy percentage: 63.7%
Life expectancy (male/female):
   42.37/48.21

SOMALIA

Capital: Mogadishu
Area (sq km): 630,000
Population: 7,253,137 (July 2000 est)
Languages: Somali, Arabic, English,
   Italian
Principal religions: Sunni Muslim
Currency: Somali shilling
GDP per capita (in US$): 169
Adult illiteracy percentage: 75%
Life expectancy (male/female):
   44.66/47.85

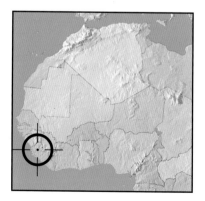

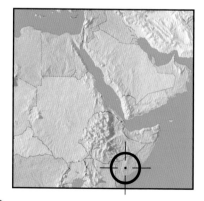

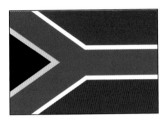

SOUTH AFRICA

Capital: Pretoria (administrative);
Cape Town (legislative)
Area (sq km): 1,220,845
Population: 43,421,021 (July 2000 est)
Languages: Afrikaans, English,
Xhosa, Zulu
Principal religions: Christian,
Dutch Reform, Roman Catholic
Currency: Rand
GDP per capita (in US$): 3,331
Adult illiteracy percentage: 14.9%
Life expectancy (male/female):
50.41/51.81

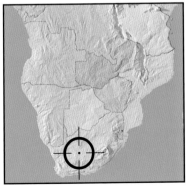

SUDAN

Capital: Khartoum
Area (sq km): 2,505,815
Population: 35,079,814 (July 2000 est)
Languages: Arabic, English, indige-
nous languages
Principal religions: Sunni Muslim,
indigenous, Christian
Currency: Sudanese dinar
GDP per capita (in US$): 59
Adult illiteracy percentage: 42.9%
Life expectancy (male/female):
55.49/57.66

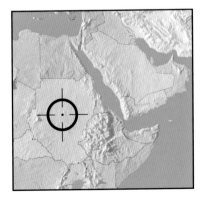

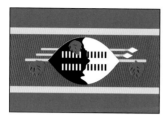

SWAZILAND

Capital: Mbabane
Area (sq km): 17,365
Population: 1,083,289 (July 2000 est)
Languages: Swazi, English
Principal religions: Christian,
  indigenous
Currency: Lilangeni
GDP per capita (in US$): 1,420
Adult illiteracy percentage: 20.2%
Life expectancy (male/female):
  39.54/41.37

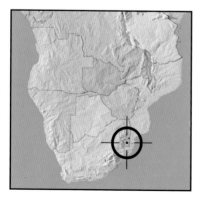

TOGO

Capital: Lome
Area (sq km): 56,785
Population: 5,018,502 (July 2000 est)
Languages: French, Ewe, Kabiye,
  Gur, Kwa
Principal religions: indigenous,
  Christian, Muslim
Currency: CFA franc
GDP per capita (in US$): 327
Adult illiteracy percentage: 42.9%
Life expectancy (male/female):
  52.75/56.7

TUNISIA

Capital: Tunis
Area (sq km): 164,150
Population: 9,593,402 (July 2000 est)
Languages: Arabic, English
Principal religions: Muslim
Currency: Tunisian dinar
GDP per capita (in US$): 2,063
Adult illiteracy percentage: 29.2%
Life expectancy (male/female):
    72.14/75.36

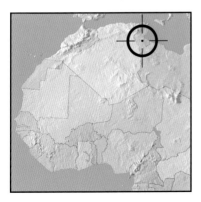

UGANDA

Capital: Kampala
Area (sq km): 235,580
Population: 23,317,560 (July 2000 est)
Languages: English, Swahili, Bantu
    languages
Principal religions: Roman
    Catholic, Protestant, indigenous,
    Muslim
Currency: Uganda shilling
GDP per capita (in US$): 313
Adult illiteracy percentage: 32.7%
Life expectancy (male/female):
    42.22/43.67

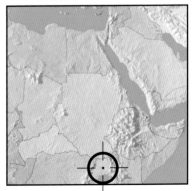

UNITED REPUBLIC OF TANZANIA

Capital: Dodoma
Area (sq km): 939,760
Population: 35,306,126 (July 2000 est)
Languages: Swahili, English
Principal religions: Christian,
Muslim, indigenous
Currency: Tanzanian shilling
GDP per capita (in US$): 245
Adult illiteracy percentage: 24.8%
Life expectancy (male/female):
51.32/53.23

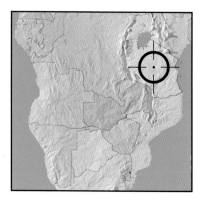

ZAIRE
(DEMOCRATIC REPUBLIC OF CONGO)

Capital: Kinshasa
Area (sq km): 2,345,410
Population: 51,964,999 (July 2000 est)
Languages: French, Swahili, Tshiluba,
Kikongo, Lingala
Principal religions: Roman Catholic,
Protestant, Kimbanguiste
Currency: New Zaire
GDP per capita (in US$): 450
Adult illiteracy percentage: 22%
Life expectancy (male/female):
46.72/50.83

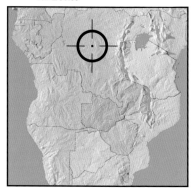

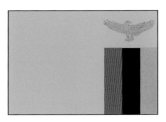

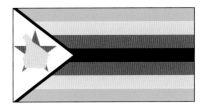

ZAMBIA

Capital: Lusaka
Area (sq km): 752,615
Population: 9,582,418 (July 2000 est)
Languages: English, Bantu languages
Principal religions: Christian,
  indigenous
Currency: Kwacha
GDP per capita (in US$): 450
Adult illiteracy percentage: 22%
Life expectancy (male/female):
  37.08/37.41

ZIMBABWE

Capital: Harare
Area (sq km): 390,310
Population: 11,342,521 (July 2000 est)
Languages: English, Shona, Ndebele
Principal religions: Christian,
  indigenous
Currency: Zimbabwe dollar
GDP per capita (in US$): 802
Adult illiteracy percentage: 7.3%
Life expectancy (male/female):
  39.18/36.34

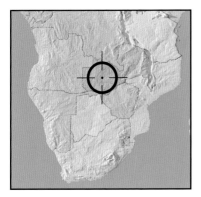

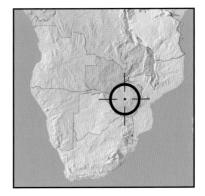

AMERICA–CENTRAL

ANTIGUA AND BARBUDA

Capital: St John's
Area (sq km): 442
Population: 66,422 (July 2000 est)
Languages: English
Principal religions: Protestant
Currency: Eastern Caribbean dollar
GDP per capita (in US$): 8,791
Adult illiteracy percentage: 4%
Life expectancy (male/female):
    68.19/72.84

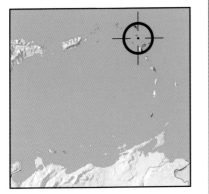

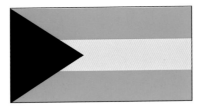

BAHAMAS

Capital: Nassau
Area (sq km): 13,865
Population: 294,982 (July 2000 est)
Languages: English, Creole
Principal religions: Protestant,
    Roman Catholic
Currency: Bahamian dollar
GDP per capita (in US$): 13,047
Adult illiteracy percentage: 3.9%
Life expectancy (male/female):
    68.25/73.94

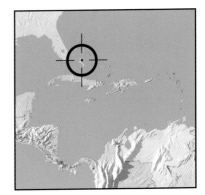

BARBADOS

Capital: Bridgetown
Area (sq km): 430
Population: 274,540 (July 2000 est)
Languages: English, Creole
Principal religions: Protestant,
Roman Catholic
Currency: Barbados dollar
GDP per capita (in US$): 8,178
Adult illiteracy percentage: 1%
Life expectancy (male/female):
70.43/75.6

BELIZE

Capital: Belmopan
Area (sq km): 22,965
Population: 249,183 (July 2000 est)
Languages: English, Creole, Spanish
Principal religions: Roman
Catholic, Protestant
Currency: Belize dollar
GDP per capita (in US$): 2,788
Adult illiteracy percentage: 5%
Life expectancy (male/female):
70.91/68.66

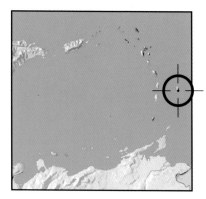

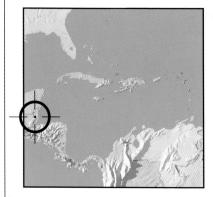

BERMUDA

Capital: Hamilton
Area (sq km): 54
Population: 62,997 (July 2000 est)
Languages: English
Principal religions: Protestant, Roman Catholic
Currency: Bermuda dollar
GDP per capita (in US$): 36,652
Adult illiteracy percentage: 2%
Life expectancy (male/female): 74.89/78.86

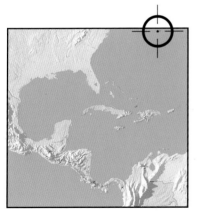

COSTA RICA

Capital: San Jose
Area (sq km): 50,900
Population: 3,710,558 (July 2000 est)
Languages: Spanish, Creole
Principal religions: Roman Catholic
Currency: Colon
GDP per capita (in US$): 2,540
Adult illiteracy percentage: 4.4%
Life expectancy (male/female): 73.3/78.47

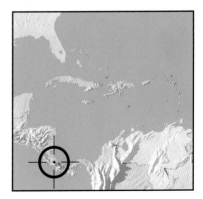

CUBA

Capital: Habana (Havana)
Area (sq km): 114,525
Population: 11,141,997 (July 2000 est)
Languages: Spanish
Principal religions: Roman
Catholic, Protestant
Currency: Cuban peso
GDP per capita (in US$): 2,100
Adult illiteracy percentage: 3.6%
Life expectancy (male/female):
73.84/78.73

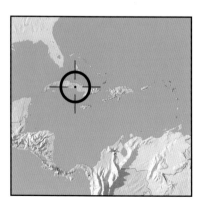

DOMINICA

Capital: Roseau
Area (sq km): 751
Population: 71,540 (July 2000 est)
Languages: English, French patois
Principal religions: Roman
Catholic, Protestant
Currency: East Caribbean dollar
GDP per capita (in US$): 3,427
Adult illiteracy percentage: 3%
Life expectancy (male/female):
70.5/76.36

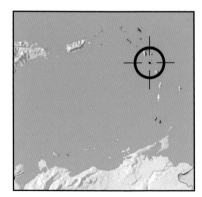

DOMINICAN REPUBLIC

Capital: Santo Domingo
Area (sq km): 48,440
Population: 8,442,533 (July 2000 est)
Languages: Spanish
Principal religions: Roman Catholic
Currency: Peso
GDP per capita (in US$): 1,841
Adult illiteracy percentage: 16.2%
Life expectancy (male/female): 71.12/75.38

EL SALVADOR

Capital: San Salvador
Area (sq km): 21,395
Population: 6,122,515 (July 2000 est)
Languages: Spanish
Principal religions: Roman Catholic, Protestant
Currency: Colon
GDP per capita (in US$): 1,935
Adult illiteracy percentage: 21.3%
Life expectancy (male/female): 66.14/73.52

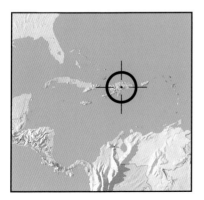

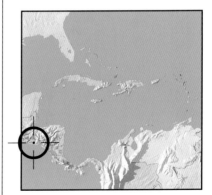

GRENADA

Capital: St George's
Area (sq km): 345
Population: 89,018 (July 2000 est)
Languages: English, French patois
Principal religions: Roman
    Catholic, Anglican, Seventh Day
    Adventist, Pentecostal
Currency: East Caribbean dollar
GDP per capita (in US$): 3,353
Adult illiteracy percentage: 4%
Life expectancy (male/female):
    62.74/66.31

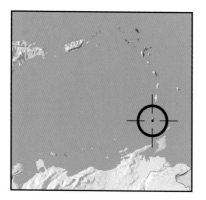

GUADELOUPE

Capital: Basse-Terre
Area (sq km): 1,780
Population: 426,493 (July 2000 est)
Languages: French, Creole
Principal religions: Roman
    Catholic
Currency: French franc
GDP per capita (in US$): 8,008
Adult illiteracy percentage: (Data
    not available)
Life expectancy (male/female):
    73.82/80.3

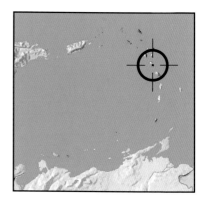

GUATEMALA

Capital: Guatemala City
Area (sq km): 108,890
Population: 12,639,939 (July 2000 est)
Languages: Spanish, Indian dialects
Principal religions: Roman
  Catholic, Pentecostal, other
  Protestant
Currency: Quetzal
GDP per capita (in US$): 1,691
Adult illiteracy percentage: 31.3%
Life expectancy (male/female):
  63.53/68.96

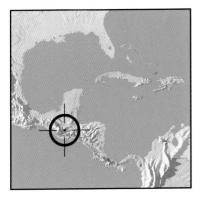

HAITI

Capital: Port-au-Prince
Area (sq km): 27,750
Population: 6,867,995 (July 2000 est)
Languages: Haitian Creole, French
Principal religions: Roman
  Catholic, other Christian,
  Voodoo
Currency: Gourde
GDP per capita (in US$): 398
Adult illiteracy percentage: 51.4%
Life expectancy (male/female):
  47.46/51.06

HONDURAS

Capital: Tegucigalpa
Area (sq km): 112,085
Population: 6,249,598 ((July 2000 est)
Languages: Spanish
Principal religions: Roman Catholic
Currency: Lempira
GDP per capita (in US$): 785
Adult illiteracy percentage: 27.8%
Life expectancy (male/female): 67.91/72.06

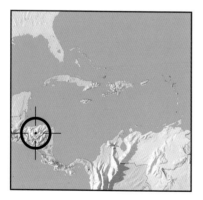

JAMAICA

Capital: Kingston
Area (sq km): 11,425
Population: 2,652,689 (July 2000 est)
Languages: English, English Creole
Principal religions: Protestant, Roman Catholic
Currency: Jamaican dollar
GDP per capita (in US$): 2,634
Adult illiteracy percentage: 13.3%
Life expectancy (male/female): 73.26/77.26

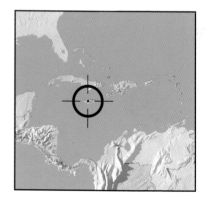

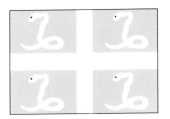

MARTINIQUE

Capital: Fort-de-France
Area (sq km): 1,079
Population: 414,516 (July 2000 est)
Languages: French, Creole
Principal religions: Roman
Catholic
Currency: French franc
GDP per capita (in US$): 11,348
Adult illiteracy percentage: 2.6%
Life expectancy (male/female):
79.03/77.46

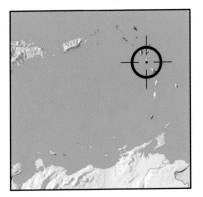

MEXICO

Capital: Mexico City
Area (sq km): 1,972,545
Population: 100,349,766 (July 2000
est)
Languages: Spanish
Principal religions: Roman
Catholic, Protestant
Currency: Peso
GDP per capita (in US$): 4,265
Adult illiteracy percentage: 9%
Life expectancy (male/female):
68.47/74.66

NETHERLANDS ANTILLES

Capital: Willemstad
Area (sq km): 800
Population: 210,134 (July 2000 est)
Languages: Dutch, English,
    Papiamento
Principal religions: Christian
Currency: Antillean guilder
GDP per capita (in US$): 13,841
Adult illiteracy percentage: 3.4%
Life expectancy (male/female):
    72.56/76.99

NICARAGUA

Capital: Managua
Area (sq km): 148,000
Population: 4,812,569 (July 2000 est)
Languages: Spanish
Principal religions: Roman
    Catholic
Currency: Cordoba
GDP per capita (in US$): 431
Adult illiteracy percentage: 35.7%
Life expectancy (male/female):
    66.81/70.77

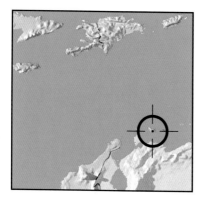

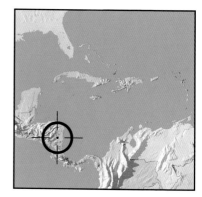

PANAMA

Capital: Panama (Panama City)
Area (sq km): 78,515
Population: 2,808,268 (July 2000 est)
Languages: Spanish, English
Principal religions: Roman Catholic
Currency: Balboa
GDP per capita (in US$): 3,159
Adult illiteracy percentage: 8.1%
Life expectancy (male/female):
72.74/78.31

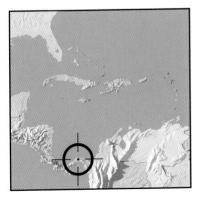

PUERTO RICO

Capital: San Juan
Area (sq km): 8,960
Population: 3,915,798 (July 2000 est)
Languages: Spanish, English
Principal religions: Roman
Catholic
Currency: US dollar
GDP per capita (in US$): 13,362
Adult illiteracy percentage: 6.2%
Life expectancy (male/female):
71.05/80.3

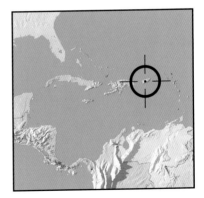

ST KITTS AND NEVIS

Capital: Basseterre
Area (sq km): 261
Population: 38,819 (July 2000 est)
Languages: English
Principal religions: Protestant,
Roman Catholic
Currency: East Caribbean dollar
GDP per capita (in US$): 6,405
Adult illiteracy percentage: 8%
Life expectancy (male/female):
67.95/73.68

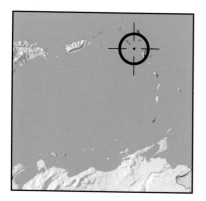

ST LUCIA

Capital: Castries
Area (sq km): 616
Population: 156,260 (July 2000 est)
Languages: English, French patois
Principal religions: Roman
Catholic, Protestant
Currency: East Caribbean dollar
GDP per capita (in US$): 4,031
Adult illiteracy percentage: 7%
Life expectancy (male/female):
68.74/76.14

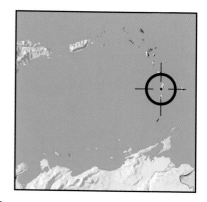

ST VINCENT AND THE GRENADINES

Capital: Kingstown
Area (sq km): 389
Population: 115,461 (July 2000 est)
Languages: English, French patois
Principal religions: Protestant,
    Roman Catholic
Currency: East Caribbean dollar
GDP per capita (in US$): 2,543
Adult illiteracy percentage: 16%
Life expectancy (male/female):
    70.6/74.06

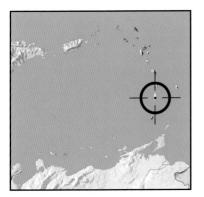

TRINIDAD AND TOBAGO

Capital: Port of Spain
Area (sq km): 5,130
Population: 1,175,523 (July 2000 est)
Languages: English
Principal religions: Roman
    Catholic, Protestant, Hindu,
    Muslim
Currency: Trinidad and Tobago
    dollar
GDP per capita (in US$): 4,397
Adult illiteracy percentage: 1.8%
Life expectancy (male/female):
    65.45/70.59

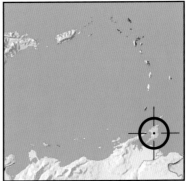

AMERICA–NORTH

CANADA

Capital: Ottawa
Area (sq km): 9,922,385
Population: 31,281,092 (July 2000 est)
Languages: English, French
Principal religions: Roman Catholic,
  Protestant
Currency: Canadian dollar
GDP per capita (in US$): 20,082
Adult illiteracy percentage: 1%
Life expectancy (male/female):
  76.02/83

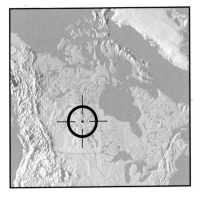

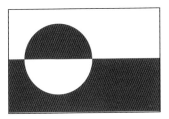

GREENLAND

Capital: Nuuk
Area (sq km): 2,175,600
Population: 56,309 (July 2000 est)
Languages: Danish, Eskimo dialects
Principal religions: Christian
Currency: Danish krone
GDP per capita (in US$): 30,718
Adult illiteracy percentage: (Data
  not available)
Life expectancy (male/female):
  64.52/71.69

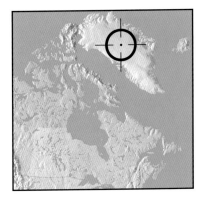

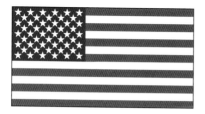

UNITED STATES

Capital: Washington, DC
Area (sq km): 9,363,130
Population: 275,562,673 (July 2000 est)
Languages: English, Spanish
Principal religions: Christian, Jewish
Currency: US dollar
GDP per capita (in US$): 28,789
Adult illiteracy percentage: 1%
Life expectancy (male/female):
74.24/79.9

ALABAMA

Capital: Montgomery
Area (sq km): 131,485
Population: 4,229,000 (1994)
Languages: English
Principal religions: Christian
Currency: US dollar
GSP per capita (in US$): 25,971 (1998)

ALASKA

Capital: Juneau
Area (sq km): 1,478,450
Population: 619,000 (1994)
Languages: English, Native North American
Principal religions: Christian
Currency: US dollar
GSP per capita (in US$): 39,153 (1998)

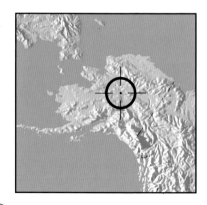

ARIZONA

Capital: Phoenix
Area (sq km): 293,985
Population: 3,994,000 (1994)
Languages: English, Spanish
Principal religions: Christian
Currency: US dollar
GSP per capita (in US$): 33,500
(1998)

ARKANSAS

Capital: Little Rock
Area (sq km): 134,880
Population: 2,445,000 (1994)
Languages: English
Principal religions: Christian
Currency: US dollar
GSP per capita (in US$): 25,205
(1998)

CALIFORNIA

Capital: Sacramento
Area (sq km): 404,815
Population: 31,902,000 (1994)
Languages: English, Spanish
Principal religions: Christian
Currency: US dollar
GSP per capita (in US$): 35,076
   (1998)

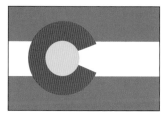

COLORADO

Capital: Denver
Area (sq km): 263,310
Population: 3,631,000 (1994)
Languages: English
Principal religions: Christian
Currency: US dollar
GSP per capita (in US$): 39,050
   (1998)

CONNECTICUT

Capital: Hartford
Area (sq km): 12,620
Population: 3,276,000 (1994)
Languages: English
Principal religions: Christian
Currency: US dollar
GSP per capita (in US$): 43,375
(1998)

DELAWARE

Capital: Dover
Area (sq km): 5,005
Population: 709,000 (1994)
Languages: English
Principal religions: Christian
Currency: US dollar
GSP per capita (in US$): 47,581
(1998)

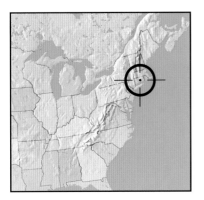

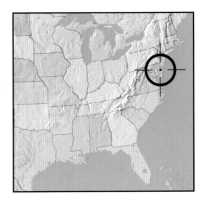

FLORIDA

GEORGIA

Capital: Tallahassee
Area (sq km): 140,255
Population: 13,973,000 (1994)
Languages: English, Spanish
Principal religions: Christian
Currency: US dollar
GSP per capita (in US$): 29,975 (1998)

Capital: Atlanta
Area (sq km): 150,365
Population: 6,987,000 (1994)
Languages: English
Principal religions: Christian
Currency: US dollar
GSP per capita (in US$): 36,320 (1998)

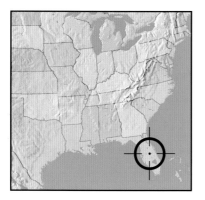

HAWAII

Capital: Honolulu
Area (sq km): 16,640
Population: 1,200,000 (1994)
Languages: English, Japanese
Principal religions: Christian
Currency: US dollar
GSP per capita (in US$): 33,093
(1998)

IDAHO

Capital: Boise
Area (sq km): 213,445
Population: 1,126,000 (1994)
Languages: English
Principal religions: Christian
Currency: US dollar
GSP per capita (in US$): 27,474
(1998)

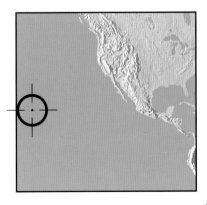

ILLINOIS

ILLINOIS

Capital: Springfield
Area (sq km): 144,120
Population: 11,782,000 (1994)
Languages: English, Spanish
Principal religions: Christian
Currency: US dollar
GSP per capita (in US$): 36,129
　　(1998)

INDIANA

Capital: Indianapolis
Area (sq km): 144,210
Population: 5,769,000 (1994)
Languages: English
Principal religions: Christian
Currency: US dollar
GSP per capita (in US$): 30,236
　　(1998)

IOWA

Capital: Des Moines
Area (sq km): 144,950
Population: 2,845,000 (1994)
Languages: English
Principal religions: Christian
Currency: US dollar
GSP per capita (in US$): 29,746
  (1998)

KANSAS

Capital: Topeka
Area (sq km): 211,805
Population: 2,575,000 (1994)
Languages: English
Principal religions: Christian
Currency: US dollar
GSP per capita (in US$): 29,899
  (1998)

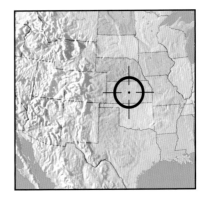

KENTUCKY

Capital: Frankfort
Area (sq km): 102,740
Population: 3,820,000 (1994)
Languages: English
Principal religions: Christian
Currency: US dollar
GSP per capita (in US$): 28,050
(1998)

LOUISIANA

Capital: Baton Rouge
Area (sq km): 115,310
Population: 4,336,000 (1994)
Languages: English, French
Principal religions: Christian
Currency: US dollar
GSP per capita (in US$): 29,808
(1998)

MAINE

Capital: Augusta
Area (sq km): 80,275
Population: 1,236,000 (1994)
Languages: English
Principal religions: Christian
Currency: US dollar
GSP per capita (in US$): 26,147
  (1998)

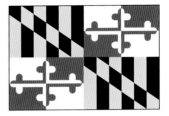

MARYLAND

Capital: Annapolis
Area (sq km): 25,480
Population: 5,023,000 (1994)
Languages: English
Principal religions: Christian
Currency: US dollar
GSP per capita (in US$): 32,808
  (1998)

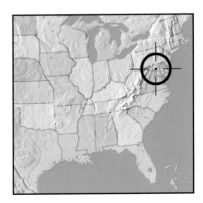

MASSACHUSETTS

Capital: Boston
Area (sq km): 20,265
Population: 5,983,000 (1994)
Languages: English
Principal religions: Christian
Currency: US dollar
GSP per capita (in US$): 40,009
(1998)

MICHIGAN

Capital: Lansing
Area (sq km): 147,510
Population: 9,531,000 (1994)
Languages: English
Principal religions: Christian
Currency: US dollar
GSP per capita (in US$): 30,899
(1998)

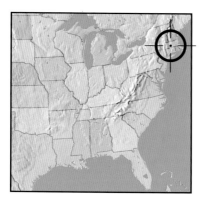

MINNESOTA

Capital: St. Paul
Area (sq km): 206,030
Population: 4,573,000 (1994)
Languages: English
Principal religions: Christian
Currency: US dollar
GSP per capita (in US$): 35,292
  (1998)

MISSISSIPPI

Capital: Jackson
Area (sq km): 122,335
Population: 2,649,000 (1994)
Languages: English
Principal religions: Christian
Currency: US dollar
GSP per capita (in US$): 23,486
  (1998)

MISSOURI

Capital: Jefferson City
Area (sq km): 178,565
Population: 5,255,000 (1994)
Languages: English
Principal religions: Christian
Currency: US dollar
GSP per capita (in US$): 30,974
(1998)

MONTANA

Capital: Helena
Area (sq km): 376,555
Population: 849,000 (1994)
Languages: English
Principal religions: Christian
Currency: US dollar
GSP per capita (in US$): 23,393
(1998)

NEBRASKA

Capital: Lincoln
Area (sq km): 198,505
Population: 1,632,000 (1994)
Languages: English
Principal religions: Christian
Currency: US dollar
GSP per capita (in US$): 31,701
(1998)

NEVADA

Capital: Carson City
Area (sq km): 284,625
Population: 1,429,000 (1994)
Languages: English, Spanish
Principal religions: Christian
Currency: US dollar
GSP per capita (in US$): 44,117
(1998)

NEW HAMPSHIRE

Capital: Concord
Area (sq km): 23,290
Population: 1,125,000 (1994)
Languages: English
Principal religions: Christian
Currency: US dollar
GSP per capita (in US$): 36,722
(1998)

NEW JERSEY

Capital: Trenton
Area (sq km): 19,340
Population: 7,885,000 (1994)
Languages: English, Spanish
Principal religions: Christian
Currency: US dollar
GSP per capita (in US$): 40,482
(1998)

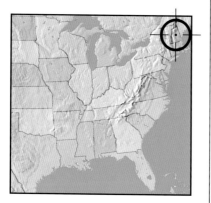

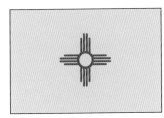

NEW MEXICO

Capital: Santa Fe
Area (sq km): 314,225
Population: 1,645,000 (1994)
Languages: English, Spanish, Native
    North American
Principal religions: Christian
Currency: US dollar
GSP per capita (in US$): 29,018
    (1998)

NEW YORK

Capital: New York
Area (sq km): 122,705
Population: 18,159,000 (1994)
Languages: English, Spanish, Italian,
    Chinese
Principal religions: Christian, Jewish
Currency: US dollar
GSP per capita (in US$): 38,927
    (1998)

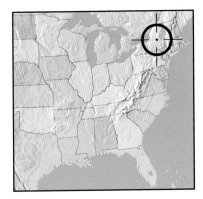

NORTH CAROLINA

Capital: Raleigh
Area (sq km): 126,505
Population: 7,049,000 (1994)
Languages: English
Principal religions: Christian
Currency: US dollar
GSP per capita (in US$): 33,444
(1998)

NORTH DAKOTA

Capital: Bismarck
Area (sq km): 179,485
Population: 637,000 (1994)
Languages: English
Principal religions: Christian
Currency: US dollar
GSP per capita (in US$): 27,023
(1998)

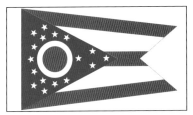

OHIO

Capital: Columbus
Area (sq km): 106,200
Population: 11,143,000 (1994)
Languages: English
Principal religions: Christian
Currency: US dollar
GSP per capita (in US$): 30,608
(1998)

OKLAHOMA

Capital: Oklahoma City
Area (sq km): 177,815
Population: 3,251,000 (1994)
Languages: English
Principal religions: Christian
Currency: US dollar
GSP per capita (in US$): 25,116
(1998)

OREGON

Capital: Salem
Area (sq km): 249,115
Population: 3,086,000 (1994)
Languages: English
Principal religions: Christian
Currency: US dollar
GSP per capita (in US$): 33,950
(1998)

PENNSYLVANIA

Capital: Harrisburg
Area (sq km): 116,260
Population: 12,093,000 (1994)
Languages: English
Principal religions: Christian
Currency: US dollar
GSP per capita (in US$): 30,103
(1998)

RHODE ISLAND

Capital: Providence
Area (sq km): 2,730
Population: 1,002,000 (1994)
Languages: English, Portuguese
Principal religions: Christian
Currency: US dollar
GSP per capita (in US$): 30,382
   (1998)

SOUTH CAROLINA

Capital: Columbia
Area (sq km): 78,225
Population: 3,690,000 (1994)
Languages: English
Principal religions: Christian
Currency: US dollar
GSP per capita (in US$): 27,195
   (1998)

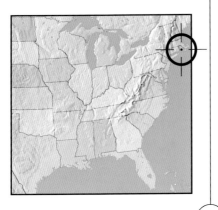

SOUTH DAKOTA

Capital: Pierre
Area (sq km): 196,715
Population: 727,000 (1994)
Languages: English
Principal religions: Christian
Currency: US dollar
GSP per capita (in US$): 29,193
(1998)

TENNESSEE

Capital: Nashville-Davidson
Area (sq km): 106,590
Population: 5,161,000 (1994)
Languages: English
Principal religions: Christian
Currency: US dollar
GSP per capita (in US$): 30,919
(1998)

TEXAS

Capital: Austin
Area (sq km): 678,620
Population: 18,291,000 (1994)
Languages: English, Spanish
Principal religions: Christian
Currency: US dollar
GSP per capita (in US$): 35,295
   (1998)

UTAH

Capital: Salt Lake City
Area (sq km): 212,570
Population: 1,901,000 (1994)
Languages: English
Principal religions: Christian
Currency: US dollar
GSP per capita (in US$): 31,364
   (1998)

VERMONT

Capital: Montpelier
Area (sq km): 24,015
Population: 576,000 (1994)
Languages: English
Principal religions: Christian
Currency: US dollar
GSP per capita (in US$): 28,223
     (1998)

VIRGINIA

Capital: Richmond
Area (sq km): 102,835
Population: 6,558,000 (1994)
Languages: English
Principal religions: Christian
Currency: US dollar
GSP per capita (in US$): 35,197
     (1998)

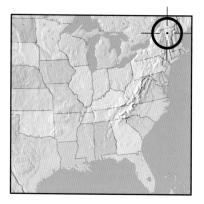

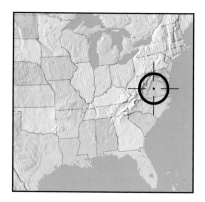

WASHINGTON

Capital: -
Area (sq km): 172,265
Population: 5,376,000 (1994)
Languages: English
Principal religions: Christian
Currency: US dollar
GSP per capita (in US$): 35,875
  (1998)

WEST VIRGINIA

Capital: Charleston
Area (sq km): 62,470
Population: 1,820,000 (1994)
Languages: English
Principal religions: Christian
Currency: US dollar
GSP per capita (in US$): 21,943
  (1998)

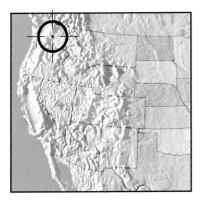

WISCONSIN

Capital: Madison
Area (sq km): 140,965
Population: 5,109,000 (1994)
Languages: English
Principal religions: Christian
Currency: US dollar
GSP per capita (in US$): 30,897
(1998)

WYOMING

Capital: Cheyenne
Area (sq km): 251,200
Population: 480,000 (1994)
Languages: English
Principal religions: Christian
Currency: US dollar
GSP per capita (in US$): 36,520
(1998)

DISTRICT OF COLUMBIA

Capital: -
Area (sq km): 163
Population: 567,000 (1994)
Languages: English
Principal religions: Christian
Currency: US dollar
GSP per capita (in US$): 95,414
(1998)

Surrounded by flags, the Washington Monument is one of the most well-known landmarks in the US.

AMERICA-SOUTH

ARGENTINA

Capital: Buenos Aires
Area (sq km): 2,777,815
Population: 36,955,182 (July 2000 est)
Languages: Spanish
Principal religions: Roman Catholic,
  Protestant
Currency: Peso
GDP per capita (in US$): 9,070
Adult illiteracy percentage: 3.1%
Life expectancy (male/female):
  69.6/76.8

BOLIVIA

Capital: La Paz
Area (sq km): 1,098,575
Population: 8,152,620 (July 2000 est)
Languages: Spanish, Aymara, Quechua
Principal religions: Roman Catholic
Currency: Boliviano
GDP per capita (in US$): 996
Adult illiteracy percentage: 14.4%
Life expectancy (male/female):
  59.8/63.2

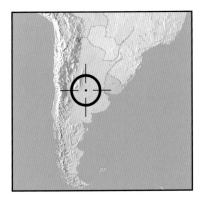

BRAZIL

Capital: Brasilia
Area (sq km): 8,511,965
Population: 172,860,370 (July 2000 est)
Languages: Portuguese, Spanish, English
Principal religions: Roman Catholic, Protestant
Currency: Cruzeiro Real
GDP per capita (in US$): 4,930
Adult illiteracy percentage: 14.7%
Life expectancy (male/female): 58.54/67.56

CHILE

Capital: Santiago
Area (sq km): 751,625
Population: 15,153,797 (July 2000 est)
Languages: Spanish
Principal religions: Roman Catholic, Protestant
Currency: Chilean peso
GDP per capita (in US$): 5,271
Adult illiteracy percentage: 4.3%
Life expectancy (male/female): 72.43/79.22

COLOMBIA

Capital: Bogota
Area (sq km): 1,138,915
Population: 39,685,655 (July 2000 est)
Languages: Spanish
Principal religions: Roman Catholic
Currency: Colombian peso
GDP per capita (in US$): 2,384
Adult illiteracy percentage: 8.2%
Life expectancy (male/female):
66.43/74.27

ECUADOR

Capital: Quito
Area (sq km): 461,475
Population: 12,920,092 (July 2000 est)
Languages: Spanish, Quechua
Principal religions: Roman Catholic,
Protestant
Currency: Sucre
GDP per capita (in US$): 1,648
Adult illiteracy percentage: 8.1%
Life expectancy (male/female):
68.26/73.99

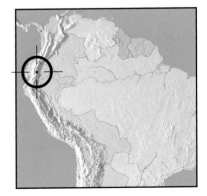

FRENCH GUIANA

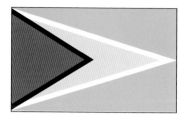

GUYANA

FRENCH GUIANA
Capital: Cayenne
Area (sq km): 91,000
Population: 172,605 (July 2000 est)
Languages: French
Principal religions: Roman Catholic
Currency: French franc
GDP per capita (in US$): 9,373
**Adult illiteracy percentage: (Data
not available)**
**Life expectancy (male/female):
72.77/79.6**

Capital: Georgetown
Area (sq km): 214,970
Population: 697,286 (July 2000 est)
Languages: English, Hindi, Urdu
Principal religions: Protestant, Hindu,
Roman Catholic, Muslim
Currency: Guyanan dollar
GDP per capita (in US$): 881
Adult illiteracy percentage: 1.5%
Life expectancy (male/female):
61.08/67.15

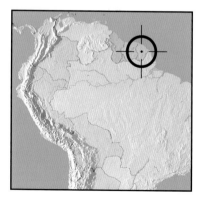

PARAGUAY

Capital: Asuncion
Area (sq km): 406,750
Population: 5,585,828 (July 2000 est)
Languages: Spanish, Guarani
Principal religions: Roman Catholic
Currency: Guarani
GDP per capita (in US$): 1,961
Adult illiteracy percentage: 6.7%
Life expectancy (male/female):
    71.22/76.27

PERU

Capital: Lima
Area (sq km): 1,285,215
Population: 27,012,899 (July 2000 est)
Languages: Spanish, Quechua, Aymara
Principal religions: Roman Catholic
Currency: Nuevo sol
GDP per capita (in US$): 2,674
Adult illiteracy percentage: 10.1%
Life expectancy (male/female):
    67.63/72.5

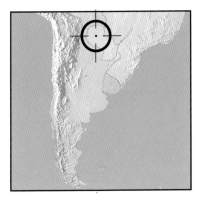

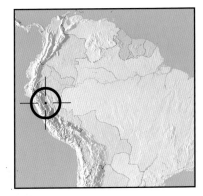

SURINAM

Capital: Paramaribo
Area (sq km): 163,820
Population: 431,303 (July 2000 est)
Languages: Dutch, Spanish, English
Principal religions: Hindu, Roman
    Catholic, Muslim, Protestant
Currency: Surinam guilder
GDP per capita (in US$): 3,733
Adult illiteracy percentage: 5.8%
Life expectancy (male/female):
    68.71/74.14

URUGUAY

Capital: Montevideo
Area (sq km): 186,925
Population: 3,334,074 (July 2000 est)
Languages: Spanish
Principal religions: Roman Catholic
Currency: Uruguayan peso
GDP per capita (in US$): 6,026
Adult illiteracy percentage: 2.2%
Life expectancy (male/female):
    71.9/78.75

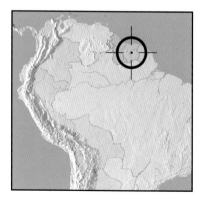

VENEZUELA

Capital: Caracas
Area (sq km): 912,045
Population: 23,542,649 (July 2000 est)
Languages: Spanish
Principal religions: Roman Catholic
Currency: Bolivar
GDP per capita (in US$): 3,678
Adult illiteracy percentage: 7%
Life expectancy (male/female):
  70.05/76.31

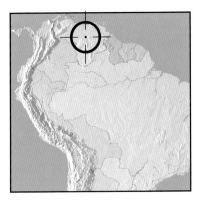

A Brazilian soccer fan with the national flag.

ASIA

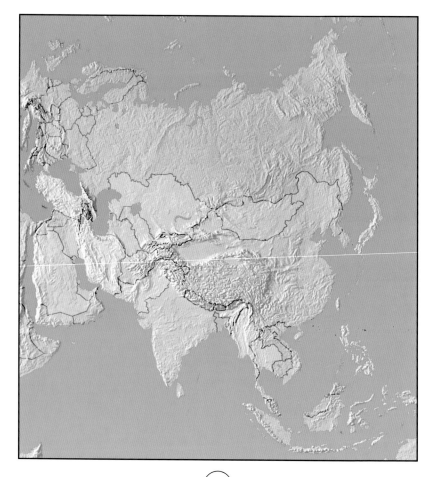

AFGHANISTAN

Capital: Kabul
Area (sq km): 652,225
Population: 25,838,797 (July 2000 est)
Languages: Pushtu, Dari
Principal religions: Sunni Muslim,
Shiite Muslim
Currency: Afghani
GDP per capita (in US$): 286
Adult illiteracy percentage: 63.7%
Life expectancy (male/female):
46.62/45.1

ARMENIA

Capital: Yerevan
Area (sq km): 30,000
Population: 3,344,336 (July 2000 est)
Languages: Armenian
Principal religions: Armenian
Orthodox
Currency: Dram
GDP per capita (in US$): 458
Adult illiteracy percentage: 7%
Life expectancy (male/female):
61.98/71.04

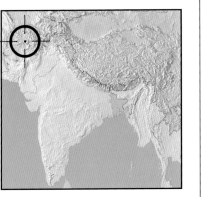

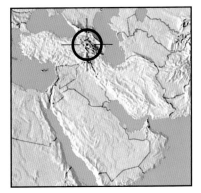

AZERBAIJAN

Capital: Baku
Area (sq km): 87,000
Population: 7,748,163 (July 2000 est)
Languages: Azerbaijani
Principal religions: Shiite Muslim,
Sunni Muslim
Currency: Manat
GDP per capita (in US$): 496
Adult illiteracy percentage: 7%
Life expectancy (male/female):
65.5/74.1

BAHRAIN

Capital: Al Manamah (Manama)
Area (sq km): 661
Population: 634,137 (July 2000 est)
Languages: Arabic
Principal religions: Shiite Muslim,
Sunni Muslim, Christian
Currency: Bahrain dinar
GDP per capita (in US$): 9,522
Adult illiteracy percentage: 12.4%
Life expectancy (male/female):
70.58/70.45

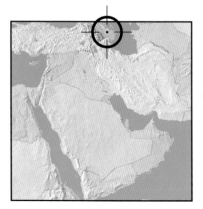

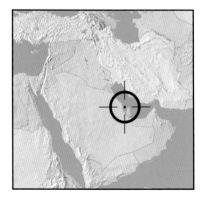

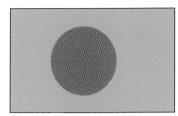

BANGLADESH

Capital: Dhaka
Area (sq km): 144,000
Population: 129,194,224 (July 2000 est)
Languages: Bengali, English
Principal religions: Sunni Muslim,
  Hindu
Currency: Taka
GDP per capita (in US$): 286
Adult illiteracy percentage: 59.2%
Life expectancy (male/female):
  60.4/59.91

BHUTAN

Capital: Thimphu
Area (sq km): 46,620
Population: 2,005,222 (July 2000 est)
Languages: Tibetan, Nepalese
Principal religions: Buddhist, Hindu
Currency: Ngultrum
GDP per capita (in US$): 197
Adult illiteracy percentage: 52.7%
Life expectancy (male/female):
  52.79/51.99

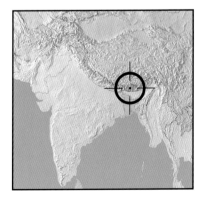

BRUNEI DARUSSALAM

Capital: Bandar Seri Begawan
Area (sq km): 5,765
Population: 336,376 (July 2000 est)
Languages: Malay, English, Chinese
Principal religions: Muslim, Buddhist,
    Christian
Currency: Brunei dollar
GDP per capita (in US$): 17,890
Adult illiteracy percentage: 8.4%
Life expectancy (male/female):
    71.23/76.06

CAMBODIA

Capital: Phnom Penh
Area (sq km): 181,000
Population: 12,212,306 (July 2000 est)
Languages: Khmer, French
Principal religions: Buddhist
Currency: Riel
GDP per capita (in US$): 159
Adult illiteracy percentage: 65%
Life expectancy (male/female):
    54.44/58.74

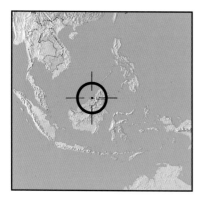

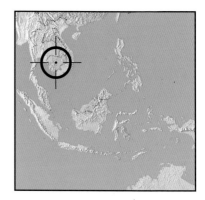

CHINA

Capital: Beijing
Area (sq km): 9,597,000
Population: 1,261,832,482 (July 2000 est)
Languages: Chinese
Principal religions: Confucian, Buddhist, Taoist, Muslim
Currency: Renminbi yuan
GDP per capita (in US$): 745
Adult illiteracy percentage: 15%
Life expectancy (male/female): 69.6/73.33

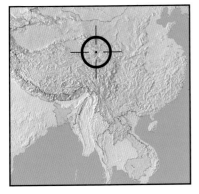

CHINA, HONG KONG SAR

Capital: Victoria
Area (sq km): 1,062
Population: 7,116,302 (July 2000 est)
Languages: Chinese, English
Principal religions: Confucian, Buddhist, Taoist, Muslim, Christian
Currency: Hong Kong dollar
GDP per capita (in US$): 26,567
Adult illiteracy percentage: 6.6%
Life expectancy (male/female): 76.85/82.41

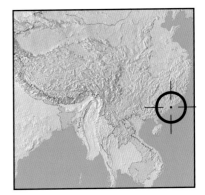

CYPRUS

Capital: Nicosia
Area (sq km): 9,250
Population: 758,363 (July 2000 est)
Languages: Greek, Turkish, English
Principal religions: Greek Orthodox, Muslim
Currency: Cyprus pound
GDP per capita (in US$): 11,106
Adult illiteracy percentage: 3.1%
Life expectancy (male/female): 74.43/79.1

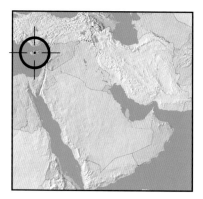

GEORGIA

Capital: Tiblisi
Area (sq km): 69,700
Population: 5,019,538 (July 2000 est)
Languages: Georgian, Armenian, Russian
Principal religions: Orthodox, Muslim
Currency: Rouble
GDP per capita (in US$): 966
Adult illiteracy percentage: (Data not available)
Life expectancy (male/female): 60.9/68.23

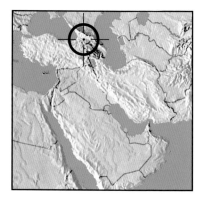

INDIA

Capital: New Delhi
Area (sq km): 3,166,830
Population: 1,014,003,817 (July 2000 est)
Languages: Hindi, English, Teluga, Bengali, Marati, Urdu
Principal religions: Hindu, Muslim, Christian, Sikh, Buddhist
Currency: Rupee
GDP per capita (in US$): 402
Adult illiteracy percentage: 44.2%
Life expectancy (male/female): 61.89/63.13

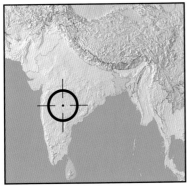

INDONESIA

Capital: Jakarta
Area (sq km): 1,919,445
Population: 224,784,210 (July 2000 est)
Languages: Bahasa Indonesian, Dutch
Principal religions: Sunni Muslim, Christian
Currency: Rupiah
GDP per capita (in US$): 1,055
Adult illiteracy percentage: 13%
Life expectancy (male/female): 65.61/70.42

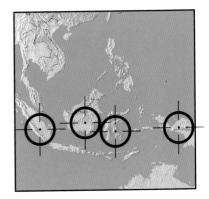

IRAN, ISLAMIC REPUBLIC OF

Capital: Tehran
Area (sq km): 1,648,000
Population: 65,619,636 (July 2000 est)
Languages: Farsi, Kurdish, Baluchi
Principal religions: Shiite Muslim
Currency: Rial
GDP per capita (in US$): 2,466
Adult illiteracy percentage: 23.1%
Life expectancy (male/female):
68.34/71.05

IRAQ

Capital: Baghdad
Area (sq km): 438,445
Population: 22,675,617 (July 2000 est)
Languages: Arabic, Kurdish, Turkish
Principal religions: Shiite Muslim,
Sunni Muslim
Currency: Dinar
GDP per capita (in US$): 7,037
Adult illiteracy percentage: 40%
Life expectancy (male/female):
65.54/67.56

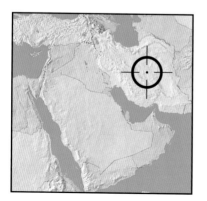

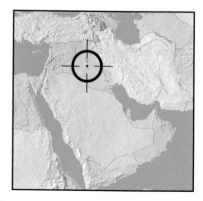

ISRAEL

Capital: Jerusalem
Area (sq km): 20,770
Population: 5,842,454 (July 2000 est)
Languages: Hebrew, Arabic, English
Principal religions: Jewish, Muslim,
    Christian
Currency: Shekel
GDP per capita (in US$): 15,800
Adult illiteracy percentage: 3.9%
Life expectancy (male/female):
    76.57/80.67

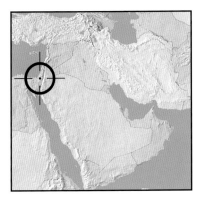

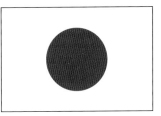

JAPAN

Capital: Tokyo
Area (sq km): 369,700
Population: 126,549,976 (July 2000 est)
Languages: Japanese, Korean, Chinese
Principal religions: Shintoism,
    Buddhism
Currency: Yen
GDP per capita (in US$): 33,265
Adult illiteracy percentage: 1%
Life expectancy (male/female):
    77.51/84.05

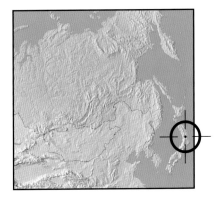

JORDAN

Capital: Amman
Area (sq km): 96,000
Population: 4,998,564 (July 2000 est)
Languages: Arabic
Principal religions: Sunni Muslim,
    Christian
Currency: Jordanian dinar
GDP per capita (in US$): 1,306
Adult illiteracy percentage: 10.2%
Life expectancy (male/female):
    74.94/79.93

KAZAKHSTAN

Capital: Alma-Ata
Area (sq km): 2,717,300
Population: 16,733,227 (July 2000 est)
Languages: Kazakh, Russian
Principal religions: Sunni Muslim,
    Christian
Currency: Tenge
GDP per capita (in US$): 1,255
Adult illiteracy percentage: (Data
    not available)
Life expectancy (male/female):
    57.73/68.93

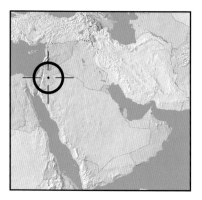

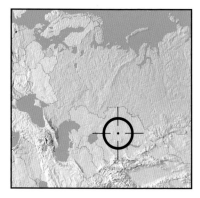

KOREA, DEMOCRATIC P R

Capital: Pyongyang
Area (sq km): 122,310
Population: 21,687,550 (July 2000 est)
Languages: Korean, Chinese
Principal religions: Chondogyo,
indigenous, Buddhist, Christian
Currency: North Korean won
GDP per capita (in US$): 232
Adult illiteracy percentage: (Data
not available)
Life expectancy (male/female):
67.76/73.86

KOREA, REPUBLIC OF

Capital: Seoul
Area (sq km): 98,445
Population: 47,470,969 (July 2000 est)
Languages: Korean
Principal religions: Buddhist,
Protestant, Roman Catholic,
Confucian
Currency: South Korean won
GDP per capita (in US$): 9,677
Adult illiteracy percentage: 2.2%
Life expectancy (male/female):
70.75/78.54

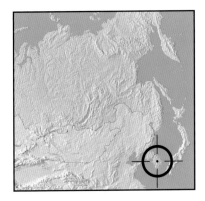

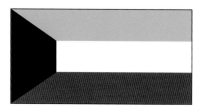

KUWAIT

Capital: Al Kuwayt (Kuwait)
Area (sq km): 24,280
Population: 1,973,572 (July 2000 est)
Languages: Arabic, English
Principal religions: Sunni Muslim,
  Shiite Muslim, Christian
Currency: Kuwaiti dinar
GDP per capita (in US$): 17,533
Adult illiteracy percentage: 17.7%
Life expectancy (male/female):
  75.27/76.92

KYRGYZSTAN

Capital: Bishkek
Area (sq km): 198,500
Population: 4,685,230 (July 2000 est)
Languages: Kirghiz
Principal religions: Sunni Muslim,
  Christian
Currency: Som
GDP per capita (in US$): 380
Adult illiteracy percentage: (Data
  not available)
Life expectancy (male/female):
  59.06/67.9

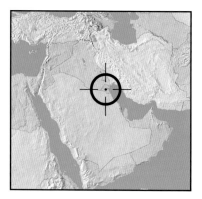

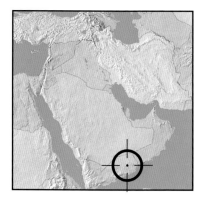

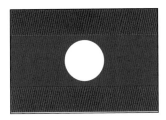

LAO PEOPLE'S DEMOCRATIC REPUBLIC

Capital: Vientiane
Area (sq km): 236,725
Population: 5,497,459 (July 2000 est)
Languages: Lao, French, English
Principal religions: Buddhist,
indigenous
Currency: Kip
GDP per capita (in US$): 348
Adult illiteracy percentage: 38.2%
Life expectancy (male/female):
51.22/55.02

LEBANON

Capital: Beyrouth (Beirut)
Area (sq km): 10,400
Population: 3,578,036 (July 2000 est)
Languages: Arabic, French, English,
Armenian
Principal religions: Shiite Muslim,
Maronite Christian, Sunni Muslim
Currency: Lebanese pound
GDP per capita (in US$): 4,546
Adult illiteracy percentage: 13.9%
Life expectancy (male/female):
68.87/73.74

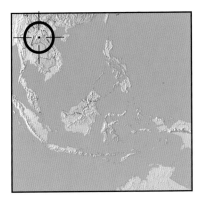

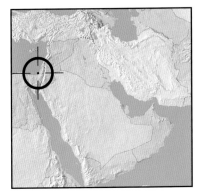

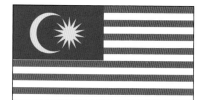

MACAU

Capital: Nome de Deus de Macau
Area (sq km): 17
Population: 445,594 (July 2000 est)
Languages: Portuguese, Chinese, English
Principal religions: Roman Catholic, Buddhist
Currency: Pataca
GDP per capita (in US$): (Data not available)
Adult illiteracy percentage: 6.8%
Life expectancy (male/female): 78.8/84.55

MALAYSIA

Capital: Kuala Lumpur
Area (sq km): 332,965
Population: 21,793,293 (July 2000 est)
Languages: Bahasa Malaysian, Chinese, Tamil, English
Principal religions: Sunni Muslim, Buddhist, Taoist, Hindu, Christian
Currency: Ringgit
GDP per capita (in US$): 4,665
Adult illiteracy percentage: 12.5%
Life expectancy (male/female): 68.22/73.63

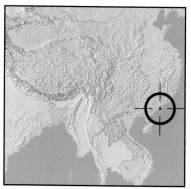

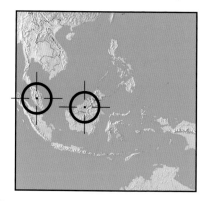

MALDIVES

Capital: Male
Area (sq km): 298
Population: 301,475 (July 2000 est)
Languages: Divehi, English, Arabic
Principal religions: Sunni Muslim
Currency: Rufiyaa
GDP per capita (in US$): 1,325
Adult illiteracy percentage: 3.7%
Life expectancy (male/female):
   61.05/63.4

MONGOLIA

Capital: Ulaanbaatar (Ulan Bator)
Area (sq km): 1,565,000
Population: 2,650,952 (July 2000 est)
Languages: Halh Mongol, Chinese,
   Russian
Principal religions: Shamanist,
   Muslim, Buddhist
Currency: Tugrik
GDP per capita (in US$): 375
Adult illiteracy percentage: 0.7%
Life expectancy (male/female):
   64.98/69.64

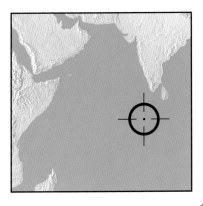

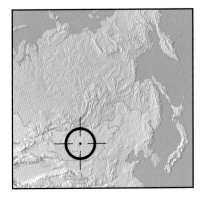

MYANMAR

Capital: Yangon (Rangoon)
Area (sq km): 678,030
Population: 41,734,853 (July 2000 est)
Languages: Burmese, English
Principal religions: Buddhist
Currency: Kyat
GDP per capita (in US$): 274
Adult illiteracy percentage: 15.3%
Life expectancy (male/female):
    53.6/56.29

NEPAL

Capital: Kathmandu
Area (sq km): 141,415
Population: 24,702,119 (July 2000 est)
Languages: Nepalese, Tibetan
Principal religions: Hindu, Buddhist
Currency: Nepalese rupee
GDP per capita (in US$): 217
Adult illiteracy percentage: 58.6%
Life expectancy (male/female):
    58.3/57.35

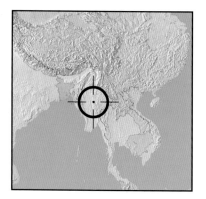

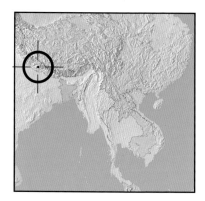

OMAN

Capital: Masqat (Muscat)
Area (sq km): 271,950
Population: 2,533,389 (July 2000 est)
Languages: Arabic, English, Baluchi
Principal religions: Muslim
Currency: Omani rial
GDP per capita (in US$): 6,751
Adult illiteracy percentage: 28.1%
Life expectancy (male/female):
    69.66/74

PAKISTAN

Capital: Islamabad
Area (sq km): 803,940
Population: 141,553,775 (July 2000 est)
Languages: Urdu, Punjabi, Sindhi,
    Baluchi, Pushtu, English
Principal religions: Muslim, Hindu,
    Christian
Currency: Pakistan rupee
GDP per capita (in US$): 466
Adult illiteracy percentage: 56.7%
Life expectancy (male/female):
    60.27/61.91

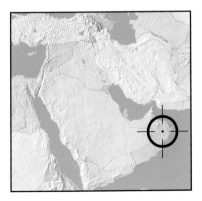

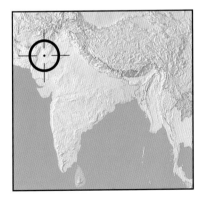

PHILIPPINES

Capital: Manila
Area (sq km): 300,000
Population: 81,159,644 (July 2000 est)
Languages: Tagalog, English
Principal religions: Roman Catholic,
　　Protestant, Sunni Muslim
Currency: Piso
GDP per capita (in US$): 1,151
Adult illiteracy percentage: 4.6%
Life expectancy (male/female):
　　64.65/70.46

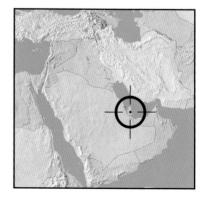

QATAR

Capital: Ad Dawhah (Doha)
Area (sq km): 11,435
Population: 744,483 (July 2000 est)
Languages: Arabic
Principal religions: Sunni Muslim
Currency: Qatari Riyal
GDP per capita (in US$): 16,166
Adult illiteracy percentage: 18.7%
Life expectancy (male/female):
　　69.92/74.94

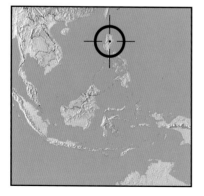

SAUDI ARABIA

Capital: Ar Riyad (Riyadh)
Area (sq km): 2,400,900
Population: 22,023,506 (July 2000 est)
Languages: Arabic
Principal religions: Sunni Muslim,
Shiite Muslim
Currency: Rial
GDP per capita (in US$): 6,921
Adult illiteracy percentage: 18%
Life expectancy (male/female):
66.11/69.51

SINGAPORE

Capital: Singapore City
Area (sq km): 616
Population: 4,151,264 (July 2000 est)
Languages: Chinese, Malay, Tamil,
English
Principal religions: Buddhist, Taoist,
Christian, Muslim, Hindu
Currency: Singapore dollar
GDP per capita (in US$): 28,107
Adult illiteracy percentage: 7.6%
Life expectancy (male/female):
77.1/83.23

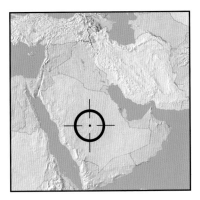

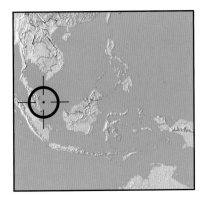

SRI LANKA

Capital: Colombo
Area (sq km): 65,610
Population: 19,238,575 (July 2000 est)
Languages: Sinhala, Tamil, English
Principal religions: Buddhist, Hindu,
    Muslim, Christian
Currency: Sri Lankan rupee
GDP per capita (in US$): 826
Adult illiteracy percentage: 8.4%
Life expectancy (male/female):
    69.33/74.45

SYRIAN ARAB REPUBLIC

Capital: Dimashq (Damascus)
Area (sq km): 185,680
Population: 16,305,659 (July 2000 est)
Languages: Arabic, Kurdish, Armenian
Principal religions: Sunni Muslim,
    Christian
Currency: Syrian pound
GDP per capita (in US$): 4,343
Adult illiteracy percentage: 25.6%
Life expectancy (male/female):
    67.35/69.94

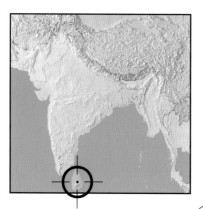

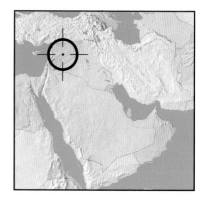

TAWIAN

Capital: Taipei
Area (sq km): 35,990
Population: 22,191,087 (July 2000 est)
Languages: Chinese
Principal religions: Buddhist, Taoist, Christian
Currency: Taiwanese dollar
GDP per capita (in US$): Data not available
Adult illiteracy percentage: Data not available
Life expectancy (male/female): 73.62/79.32

TAJIKISTAN

Capital: Dushanbe
Area (sq km): 143,100
Population: 6,440,732 (July 2000 est)
Languages: Tajik, Uzbek, Russian
Principal religions: Sunni Muslim
Currency: Rouble
GDP per capita (in US$): 178
Adult illiteracy percentage: 0.8%
Life expectancy (male/female): 60.95/67.38

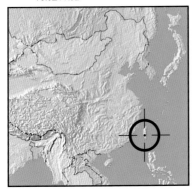

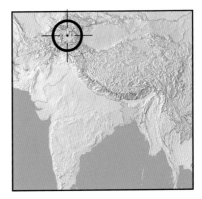

THAILAND

Capital: Bangkok (Krung Thep)
Area (sq km): 514,000
Population: 61,230,874 (July 2000 est)
Languages: Tahi, Lao, Chinese, Malay, English
Principal religions: Buddhist, Muslim
Currency: Baht
GDP per capita (in US$): 2,576
Adult illiteracy percentage: 4.4%
Life expectancy (male/female): 65.29/71.97

TURKEY

Capital: Ankara
Area (sq km): 779,450
Population: 65,666,677 (July 2000 est)
Languages: Turkish, Kurdish
Principal religions: Sunni Muslim, Shiite Muslim
Currency: Turkish lira
GDP per capita (in US$): 3,026
Adult illiteracy percentage: 14.8%
Life expectancy (male/female): 68.63/73.41

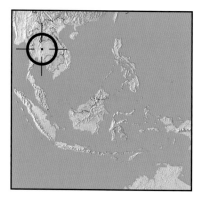

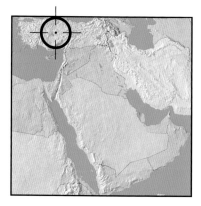

TURKMENISTAN

Capital: Ashkhabad
Area (sq km): 488,100
Population: 4,518,268 (July 2000 est)
Languages: Turkmen, Russian
Principal religions: Muslim
Currency: Manat
GDP per capita (in US$): 188
Adult illiteracy percentage: Data not available
Life expectancy (male/female): 57.29/64.71

UNITED ARAB EMIRATES

Capital: Abu Dhabi
Area (sq km): 75,150
Population: 2,369,153 (July 2000 est)
Languages: Arabic, English
Principal religions: Sunni Muslim
Currency: Dirham
GDP per capita (in US$): 20,203
Adult illiteracy percentage: 23.5%
Life expectancy (male/female): 71.64/76.61

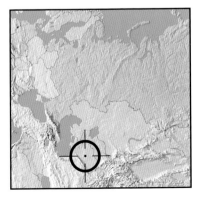

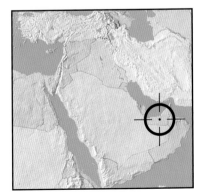

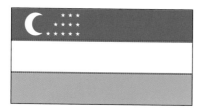

UZBEKISTAN

Capital: Tashkent
Area (sq km): 447,400
Population: 24,755,519 (July 2000 est)
Languages: Uzbek, Russian, Tajik
Principal religions: Sunni Muslim
Currency: Rouble
GDP per capita (in US$): 426
Adult illiteracy percentage: (Data not available)
Life expectancy (male/female): 60.09/67.52

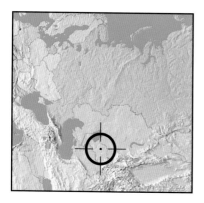

VIETNAM

Capital: Hanoi
Area (sq km): 329,565
Population: 78,773,873 (July 2000 est)
Languages: Vietnamese, French
Principal religions: Buddhist, Roman Catholic, Taoist
Currency: Dong
GDP per capita (in US$): 330
Adult illiteracy percentage: 6.7%
Life expectancy (male/female): 66.84/71.87

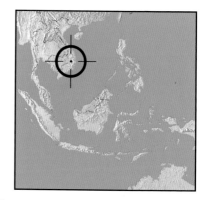

YEMEN

Capital: San'a
Area (sq km): 527,970
Population: 17,479,206 (July 2000 est)
Languages: Arabic
Principal religions: Sunni Muslim,
Shiite Muslim
Currency: North Yemeni riyal and
South Yemeni dinar
GDP per capita (in US$): 318
Adult illiteracy percentage: 53.8%
Life expectancy (male/female):
58.1/61.64

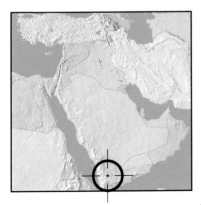

The Japanese flag over a karate competition.

217

EUROPE

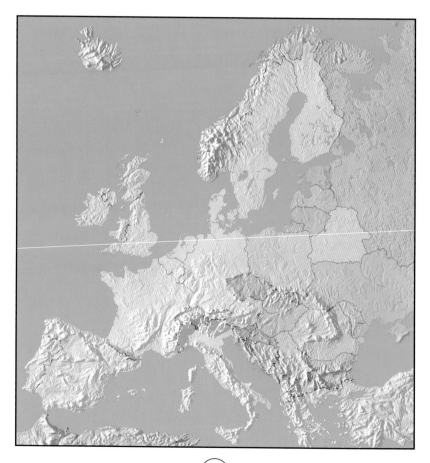

ALBANIA

Capital: Tirane (Tirana)
Area (sq km): 28,750
Population: 3,490,435 (July 2000 est)
Languages: Albanian, Greek, English
Principal religions: Sunni Muslim,
    Orthodox, Roman Catholic
Currency: Lek
GDP per capita (in US$): 723
Adult illiteracy percentage: 15%
Life expectancy (male/female):
    68.75/74.59

ANDORRA

Capital: Andorra la Vella
Area (sq km): 465
Population: 66,824 (July 2000 est)
Languages: Catalan, Spanish, French
Principal religions: Roman Catholic
Currency: French franc, Spanish peseta
GDP per capita (in US$): 13,670
Adult illiteracy percentage: 2.3
Life expectancy (male/female):
    80.56/86.56

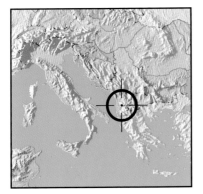

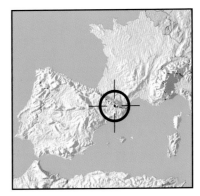

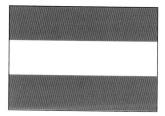

AUSTRIA

Capital: Wien (Vienna)
Area (sq km): 83,855
Population: 8,131,111 (July 2000 est)
Languages: German
Principal religions: Roman Catholic,
Protestant
Currency: Schilling
GDP per capita (in US$): 25,465
Adult illiteracy percentage: 1%
Life expectancy (male/female):
74.52/80.99

AZORES

Capital: Ponta Delgada
Area (sq km): 2,335
Population: 237,800 (July 2000 est)
Languages: Portuguese
Principal religions: Roman Catholic
Currency: Escudo
GDP per capita (in US$): (Data not
available)
Adult illiteracy percentage: (Data
not available)
Life expectancy (male/female):
(Data not available)

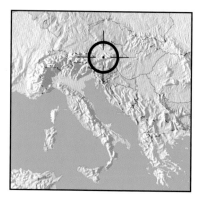

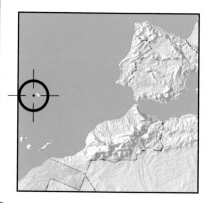

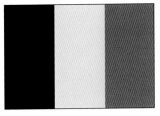

BELARUS

Capital: Minsk
Area (sq km): 208,000
Population: 10,366,719 (July 2000 est)
Languages: Belorussian, Russian
Principal religions: Christian
  Orthodox, Roman Catholic
Currency: Rouble
GDP per capita (in US$): 1,331
Adult illiteracy percentage: 0.6%
Life expectancy (male/female):
  61.83/74.48

BELGIUM

Capital: Bruxelles/Brussel (Brussels)
Area (sq km): 30,520
Population: 10,241,506 (July 2000 est)
Languages: Flemish, Dutch, French
Principal religions: Roman Catholic,
  Protestant
Currency: Belgian franc
GDP per capita (in US$): 23,948
Adult illiteracy percentage: 1%
Life expectancy (male/female):
  74.47/81.3

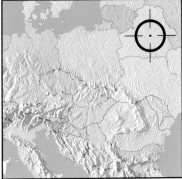

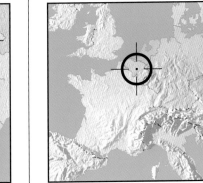

BOSNIA AND HERZEGOVINA

Capital: Sarajevo
Area (sq km): 51,130
Population: 3,835,777 (July 2000 est)
Languages: Serbo-Croat
Principal religions: Muslim,
　　Orthodox, Roman Catholic
Currency: Dinar
GDP per capita (in US$): 938
Adult illiteracy percentage: 14%
Life expectancy (male/female):
　　68.67/74.38

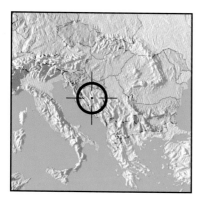

BULGARIA

Capital: Sofiya (Sofia)
Area (sq km): 110,910
Population: 7,796,694 (July 2000 est)
Languages: Bulgarian, Turkish, Romany
Principal religions: Eastern
　　Orthodox, Sunni Muslim
Currency: Lev
GDP per capita (in US$): 1,212
Adult illiteracy percentage: 1.5%
Life expectancy (male/female):
　　67.45/74.56

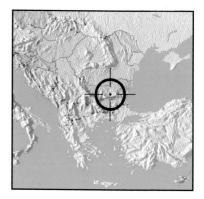

CROATIA

Capital: Zagreb
Area (sq km): 56,540
Population: 4,282,216 (July 2000 est)
Languages: Serbo-Croat
Principal religions: Roman Catholic,
Orthodox
Currency: Croatian dinar
GDP per capita (in US$): 4,352
Adult illiteracy percentage: 1.7%
Life expectancy (male/female):
70.04/77.51

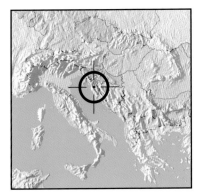

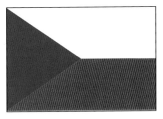

CZECH REPUBLIC

Capital: Praha (Prague)
Area (sq km): 78,864
Population: 10,272,179 (July 2000 est)
Languages: Czech
Principal religions: Protestant
Currency: Koruna
GDP per capita (in US$): 5,052
Adult illiteracy percentage: 1%
Life expectancy (male/female):
71.01/78.22

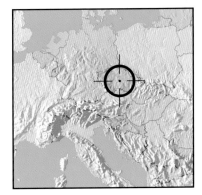

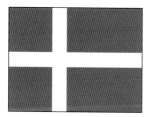

DENMARK

Capital: Kobenhaven (Copenhagen)
Area (sq km): 43,075
Population: 5,336,394 (July 2000 est)
Languages: Danish
Principal religions: Lutheran
Currency: Krone
GDP per capita (in US$): 30,718
Adult illiteracy percentage: 1%
Life expectancy (male/female):
73.95/79.27

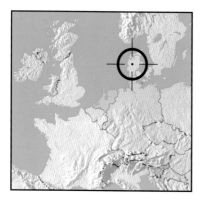

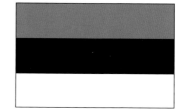

ESTONIA

Capital: Talinn
Area (sq km): 45,100
Population: 1,431,471 (July 2000 est)
Languages: Estonian, Russian
Principal religions: Lutheran,
Orthodox
Currency: Kroon
GDP per capita (in US$): 3,239
Adult illiteracy percentage: Data
not available
Life expectancy (male/female):
63.4/75.79

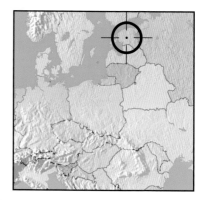

FINLAND

Capital: Helsinki
Area (sq km): 337,030
Population: 5,167,486 (July 2000 est)
Languages: Finnish, Swedish
Principal religions: Lutheran
Currency: Markka
GDP per capita (in US$): 23,309
Adult illiteracy percentage: 1%
Life expectancy (male/female):
   73.74/81.2

FRANCE

Capital: Paris
Area (sq km): 543,965
Population: 59,329,691 (July 2000 est)
Languages: French
Principal religions: Roman Catholic,
   other Christian, Muslim
Currency: Franc
GDP per capita (in US$): 23,843
Adult illiteracy percentage: 1%
Life expectancy (male/female):
   74.85/82.89

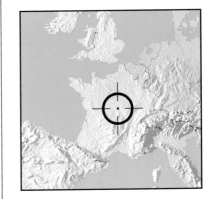

GERMANY

Capital: Berlin
Area (sq km): 356,850
Population: 82,797,408 (July 2000 est)
Languages: German
Principal religions: Protestant, Roman
   Catholic
Currency: Deutschmark
GDP per capita (in US$): 25,468
Adult illiteracy percentage: 1%
Life expectancy (male/female):
   74.3/80.75

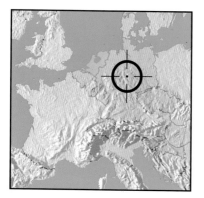

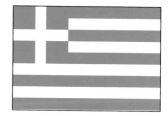

GREECE

Capital: Athinai (Athens)
Area (sq km): 131,985
Population: 10,601,527 (July 2000 est)
Languages: Greek
Principal religions: Greek Orthodox
Currency: Drachma
GDP per capita (in US$): 11,181
Adult illiteracy percentage: 2.8%
Life expectancy (male/female):
   75.89/81.16

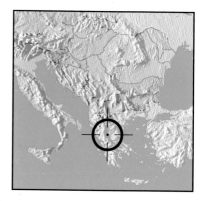

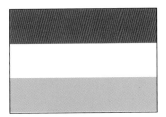

HUNGARY

Capital: Budapest
Area (sq km): 93,030
Population: 10,138,844 (July 2000 est)
Languages: Hungarian, Slovak, German
Principal religions: Roman Catholic, Protestant
Currency: Forint
GDP per capita (in US$): 4,502
Adult illiteracy percentage: 0.6%
Life expectancy (male/female): 67/76.05

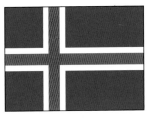

ICELAND

Capital: Reykjavik
Area (sq km): 102,820
Population: 276,365 (July 2000 est)
Languages: Icelandic
Principal religions: Lutheran
Currency: Krona
GDP per capita (in US$): 27,181
Adult illiteracy percentage: 1%
Life expectancy (male/female): 77.19/81.77

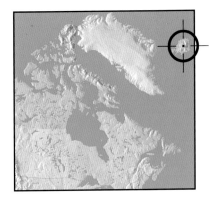

IRELAND
REPUBLIC OF (EIRE)

Capital: Dublin (Baile Atha Cliath)
Area (sq km): 68,895
Population: 3,797,257 (July 2000 est)
Languages: Irish, English
Principal religions: Roman Catholic,
 Protestant
Currency: Punt
GDP per capita (in US$): 20,603
Adult illiteracy percentage: 1%
Life expectancy (male/female):
 74.06/79.74

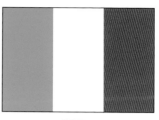

ITALY

Capital: Roma (Rome)
Area (sq km): 301,245
Population: 57,634,327 (July 2000 est)
Languages: Italian
Principal religions: Roman Catholic
Currency: Lira
GDP per capita (in US$): 19,962
Adult illiteracy percentage: 1.5%
Life expectancy (male/female):
 75.85/82.41

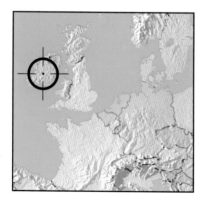

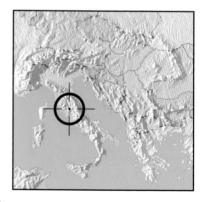

LATVIA

Capital: Riga
Area (sq km): 63,700
Population: 2,404,926 (July 2000 est)
Languages: Latvian, Russian
Principal religions: Lutheran
Currency: Lat
GDP per capita (in US$): 2,246
Adult illiteracy percentage: 0.3%
Life expectancy (male/female):
   62.48/74.62

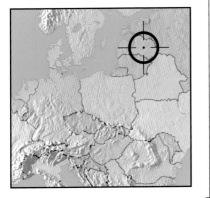

LIECHTENSTEIN

Capital: Vaduz
Area (sq km): 160
Population: 32,207 (July 2000 est)
Languages: German
Principal religions: Roman Catholic,
   Protestant
Currency: Swiss franc
GDP per capita (in US$): 35,170
Adult illiteracy percentage: 1%
Life expectancy (male/female):
   75.16/82.47

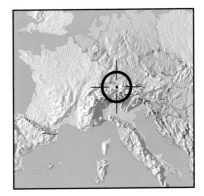

LITHUANIA

Capital: Vilnius
Area (sq km): 65,2000
Population: 3,620,756 (July 2000 est)
Languages: Lithuanian, Russian
Principal religions: Roman Catholic,
Lutheran
Currency: Litas
GDP per capita (in US$): 2,578
Adult illiteracy percentage: 0.5%
Life expectancy (male/female):
63.07/75.41

LUXEMBOURG

Capital: Luxembourg
Area (sq km): 2,585
Population: 437,389 (July 2000 est)
Languages: Letzeburgish, French,
German
Principal religions: Roman Catholic
Currency: Luxembourg franc
GDP per capita (in US$): 35,785
Adult illiteracy percentage: 0%
Life expectancy (male/female):
73.84/80.63

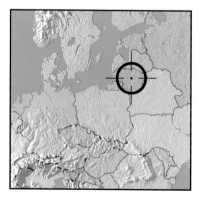

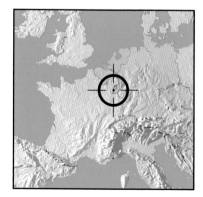

MACEDONIA

Capital: Skopje
Area (sq km): 25,715
Population: 2,041,467 (July 2000 est)
Languages: Macedonian, Albanian
Principal religions: Orthodox, Muslim
Currency: Dinar
GDP per capita (in US$): 1,671
Adult illiteracy percentage: 11%
Life expectancy (male/female):
  71.58/76.19

MALTA

Capital: Valletta
Area (sq km): 316
Population: 391,670 (July 2000 est)
Languages: Maltese, English
Principal religions: Roman Catholic
Currency: Maltese Lira
GDP per capita (in US$): 8,718
Adult illiteracy percentage: 7.9%
Life expectancy (male/female):
  75.49/80.62

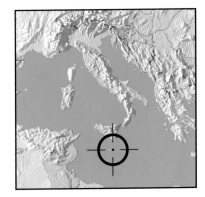

MOLDOVA
REPUBLIC OF

Capital: Kishinev
Area (sq km): 33,700
Population: 4,430,654 (July 2000 est.)
Languages: Moldavian, Russian
Principal religions: Russian Orthodox, Evangelical
Currency: Leu
GDP per capita (in US$): 428
Adult illiteracy percentage: 1.1%
Life expectancy (male/female): 59.92/69.22

MONACO

Capital: Monte Carlo
Area (sq km): 1.6
Population: 31,693 (July 2000 est)
Languages: French, Monegasque
Principal religions: Roman Catholic
Currency: French franc
GDP per capita (in US$): 23,843
Adult illiteracy percentage: 1%
Life expectancy (male/female): 74.88/83

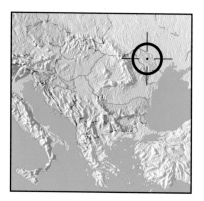

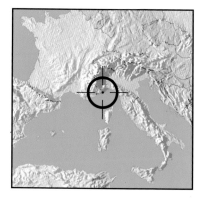

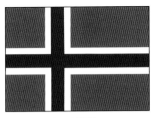

NETHERLANDS

Capital: Amsterdam (seat of government The Hague)
Area (sq km): 41,160
Population: 15,892,237 (July 2000 est)
Languages: Dutch
Principal religions: Roman Catholic, Protestant
Currency: Guilder
GDP per capita (in US$): 23,270
Adult illiteracy percentage: 1%
Life expectancy (male/female): 75.4/81.28

NORWAY

Capital: Oslo
Area (sq km): 323,895
Population: 4,481,162 (July 2000 est)
Languages: Norwegian, Lappish, Finnish
Principal religions: Lutheran, Roman Catholic
Currency: Norwegian krone
GDP per capita (in US$): 34,890
Adult illiteracy percentage: 1%
Life expectancy (male/female): 75.73/81.77

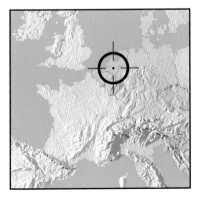

POLAND

Capital: Warszawa (Warsaw)
Area (sq km): 312,685
Population: 38,646,023 (July 2000 est)
Languages: Polish
Principal religions: Roman Catholic
Currency: Zloty
GDP per capita (in US$): 3,505
Adult illiteracy percentage: 0.2%
Life expectancy (male/female):
69.01/77.6

PORTUGAL

Capital: Lisboa (Lisbon)
Area (sq km): 91,600
Population: 10,048,232 (July 2000 est)
Languages: Portuguese
Principal religions: Roman Catholic
Currency: Escudo
GDP per capita (in US$): 10,269
Adult illiteracy percentage: 7.8%
Life expectancy (male/female):
72.24/79.49

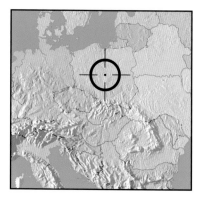

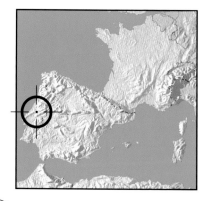

ROMANIA

Capital: Bucuresti (Bucharest)
Area (sq km): 237,500
Population: 22,411,121 (July 2000 est)
Languages: Romanian, Hungarian, German
Principal religions: Romanian Orthodox, Roman Catholic
Currency: Leu
GDP per capita (in US$): 1,545
Adult illiteracy percentage: 1.8%
Life expectancy (male/female): 66.1/73.99

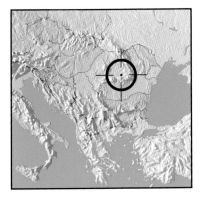

RUSSIAN FEDERATION

Capital: Moskva (Moscow)
Area (sq km): 17,078,005
Population: 146,001,176 (July 2000 est)
Languages: Russian
Principal religions: Orthodox, Muslim, Buddhist
Currency: Rouble
GDP per capita (in US$): 3,028
Adult illiteracy percentage: 0.6%
Life expectancy (male/female): 61.95/72.69

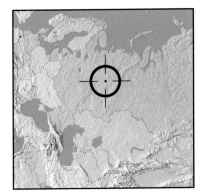

SAN MARINO

Capital: San Marino
Area (sq km): 61
Population: 26,937 (July 2000 est)
Languages: Italian
Principal religions: Roman Catholic
Currency: Italian lira
GDP per capita (in US$): 19,962
Adult illiteracy percentage: 4%
Life expectancy (male/female):
  77.57/85.02

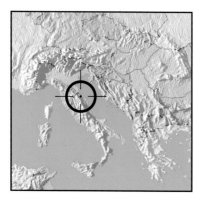

SLOVAKIA

Capital: Bratislava
Area (sq km): 49,035
Population: 5,407,956 (July 2000 est)
Languages: Slovak
Principal religions: Roman Catholic
Currency: Slovak Koruna
GDP per capita (in US$): 3,621
Adult illiteracy percentage: 1%
Life expectancy (male/female):
  69.71/77.98

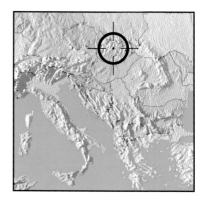

SLOVENIA

Capital: Ljubjiana
Area (sq km): 20,250
Population: 1,927,593 (July 2000 est)
Languages: Slovene, Serbo-Croat
Principal religions: Roman Catholic
Currency: Slovene Tolar
GDP per capita (in US$): 9,122
Adult illiteracy percentage: 0.3%
Life expectancy (male/female):
  70.97/78.97

SPAIN

Capital: Madrid
Area (sq km): 504,880
Population: 39,996,671 (July 2000 est)
Languages: Spanish, Catalan, Basque,
  Galician
Principal religions: Roman Catholic
Currency: Peseta
GDP per capita (in US$): 13,412
Adult illiteracy percentage: 2.3%
Life expectancy (male/female):
  75.32/82.49

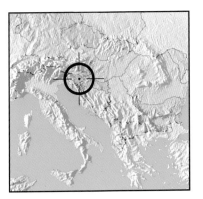

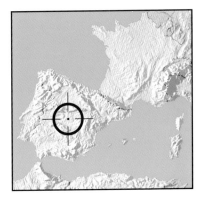

SWEDEN

Capital: Stockholm
Area (sq km): 449,790
Population: 8,873,052 (July 2000 est)
Languages: Swedish, Finnish
Principal religions: Lutheran
Currency: Krona
GDP per capita (in US$): 25,718
Adult illiteracy percentage: 1%
Life expectancy (male/female):
76.95/82.37

SWITZERLAND

Capital: Bern (Berne)
Area (sq km): 41,285
Population: 7,262,372 (July 2000 est)
Languages: German, French, Italian,
Romansch
Principal religions: Protestant, Roman
Catholic
Currency: Swiss franc
GDP per capita (in US$): 35,170
Adult illiteracy percentage: 1%
Life expectancy (male/female):
76.73/82.63

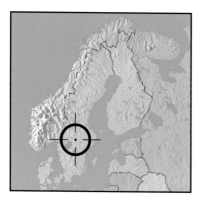

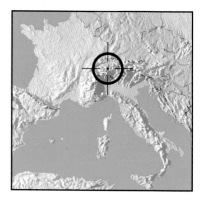

UKRAINE

Capital: Kiev
Area (sq km): 603,700
Population: 49,153,027 (July 2000 est)
Languages: Ukrainian, Russian
Principal religions: Ukrainian
   Orthodox, Roman Catholic
Currency: Rouble
GDP per capita (in US$): 973
Adult illiteracy percentage: (Data
   not available)
Life expectancy (male/female):
   60.39/71.85

UNITED KINGDOM

Capital: London
Area (sq km): 244,755
Population: 59,511,464 (July 2000 est)
Languages: English
Principal religions: Anglican, Roman
   Catholic
Currency: Pound sterling
GDP per capita (in US$): 21,921
Adult illiteracy percentage: 1%
Life expectancy (male/female):
   74.97/80.49

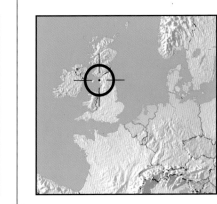

The British Union Jack flies over the Tower of London.

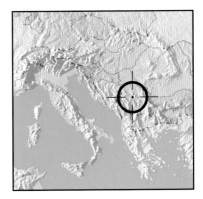

YUGOSLAVIA

Capital: Beograd (Belgrade)
Area (sq km): 102,170
Population: 10,515,000 (July 2000 est)
Languages: Serbo-Croat
Principal religions: Orthodox, Muslim
Currency: Dinar
GDP per capita (in US$): 1,600
Adult illiteracy percentage: 11%
Life expectancy (male/female):
70.2/75.5

OCEANIA

AUSTRALIA

Capital: Canberra
Area (sq km): 7,682,300
Population: 19,169,083 (July 2000 est)
Languages: English
Principal religions: Catholic, Anglican, other Christian
Currency: Australian dollar
GDP per capita (in US$): 21,971
Adult illiteracy percentage: 1%
Life expectancy (male/female): 76.9/82.74

COOK ISLANDS

Capital: Avarua on Rarotonga
Area (sq km): 233
Population: 20,407 (July 2000 est)
Languages: English
Principal religions: Christian
Currency: Cook Island dollar
GDP per capita (in US$): 5,213
Adult illiteracy percentage: (Data not available)
Life expectancy (male/female): 69.2/73.1

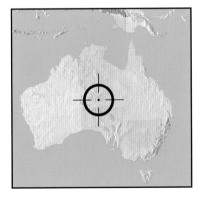

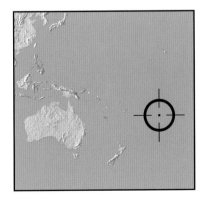

FIJI

Capital: Suva
Area (sq km): 18,330
Population: 832,494 (July 2000 est)
Languages: English, Bauan, Hindustani
Principal religions: Christian, Hindu,
Muslim
Currency: Fiji dollar
GDP per capita (in US$): 2,733
Adult illiteracy percentage: 7.1%
Life expectancy (male/female):
65.54/70.45

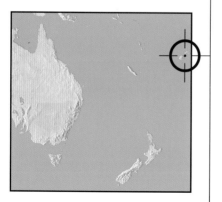

FRENCH POLYNESIA

Capital: Papeete
Area (sq km): 3,940
Population: 249,110 (July 2000 est)
Languages: French, Tahitian
Principal religions: Protestant, Roman
Catholic
Currency: CFP franc
GDP per capita (in US$): 16,646
Adult illiteracy percentage: 2%
Life expectancy (male/female):
72.47/77.22

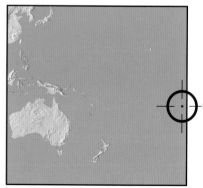

GUAM

Capital: Agana
Area (sq km): 450
Population: 154,623 (July 2000 est)
Languages: Chamorro, English
Principal religions: Roman Catholic
Currency: US dollar
GDP per capita (in US$): (Data not available)
Adult illiteracy percentage: (Data not available)
Life expectancy (male/female): 75.51/80.37

KIRIBATI

Capital: Bairiki
Area (sq km): 684
Population: 91,985 (July 2000 est)
Languages: English, Gilbertese
Principal religions: Roman Catholic, Protestant
Currency: Australian dollar
GDP per capita (in US$): 680
Adult illiteracy percentage: (Data not available)
Life expectancy (male/female): 56.89/62.82

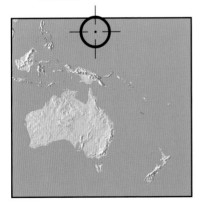

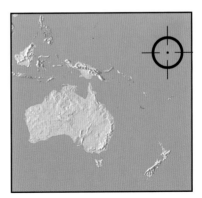

MARSHALL ISLANDS

Capital: Majuro
Area (sq km): 181
Population: 68,126 (July 2000 est)
Languages: Marshallese, English
Principal religions: Protestant
Currency: US dollar
GDP per capita (in US$): 1,661
Adult illiteracy percentage: 61/64
Life expectancy (male/female):
   59.1/63

MICRONESIA

Capital: Palikir
Area (sq km): 702
Population: 133,144 (July 2000 est)
Languages: English
Principal religions: Christian
Currency: US dollar
GDP per capita (in US$): 1,899
Adult illiteracy percentage: 22%
Life expectancy (male/female):
   66.67/70.62

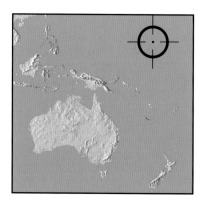

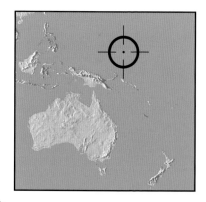

NAURU

Capital: Yaren
Area (sq km): 21
Population: 11,845 (July 2000 est)
Languages: English, Nauruan
Principal religions: Roman
Catholic, Protestant
Currency: Australian dollar
GDP per capita (in US$): 49,519
Adult illiteracy percentage: (Data
not available)
Life expectancy (male/female):
57.35/64.5

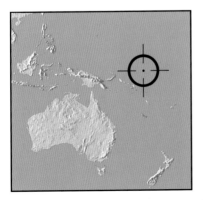

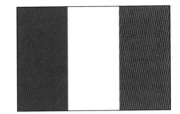

NEW CALEDONIA

Capital: Noumea
Area (sq km): 19,105
Population: 201,816 (July 2000 est)
Languages: French, English
Principal religions: Roman
Catholic
Currency: French Pacific franc
GDP per capita (in US$): 17,623
Adult illiteracy percentage: (Data
not available)
Life expectancy (male/female):
69.84/75.85

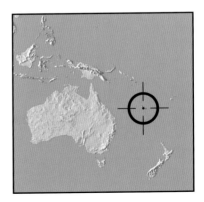

NEW ZEALAND

Capital: Wellington
Area (sq km): 265,150
Population: 3,819,762 (July 2000 est)
Languages: English, Maori
Principal religions: Protestant,
  Roman Catholic
Currency: New Zealand dollar
GDP per capita (in US$): 17,359
Adult illiteracy percentage: 1%
Life expectancy (male/female):
  77.82/74.85

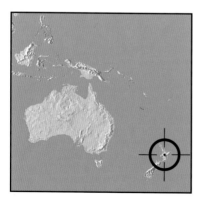

NIUE

Capital: Alofi
Area (sq km): 259
Population: 2,113 (July 2000 est)
Languages: English, Niuean
Principal religions: Christian
Currency: New Zealand dollar
GDP per capita (in US$): (Data
  not available)
Adult illiteracy percentage: (Data
  not available)
Life expectancy (male/female):
  (Data not available)

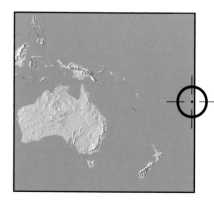

NORTHERN MARIANA ISLANDS

Capital: Saipan
Area (sq km): 471
Population: 71,912 (July 2000 est)
Languages: English, Chamorro
Principal religions: Roman
   Catholic
Currency: US dollar
GDP per capita (in US$): (Data
   not available)
Adult illiteracy percentage: 4%
Life expectancy (male/female):
   65/70

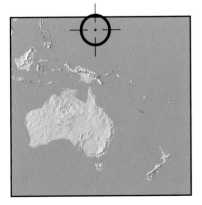

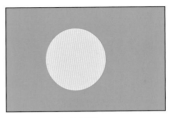

PALAU

Capital: Koror
Area (sq km): 365
Population: 18,766 (July 2000 est)
Languages: English, Palauan
Principal religions: Roman
   Catholic
Currency: US dollar
GDP per capita (in US$): 5,811
Adult illiteracy percentage: (Data
   not available)
Life expectancy (male/female):
   65.47/71.88

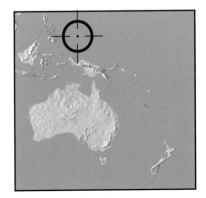

PAPUA NEW GUINEA

Capital: Port Moresby
Area (sq km): 462,840
Population: 4,926,984 (July 2000 est)
Languages: English, Aira Motu,
  Pidgin
Principal religions: Protestant,
  Roman Catholic, indigenous
Currency: Kina
GDP per capita (in US$): 1,031
Adult illiteracy percentage: 24%
Life expectancy (male/female):
  61.05/65.26

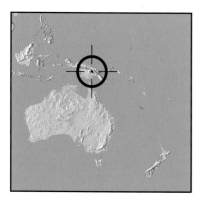

SOLOMON ISLANDS

Capital: Honiara
Area (sq km): 29,790
Population: 466,194 (July 2000 est)
Languages: English, various
  Melanesian, Papuan and
  Polynesian languages
Principal religions: Protestant,
  Roman Catholic
Currency: Solomon Island dollar
GDP per capita (in US$): 845
Adult illiteracy percentage: 76%
Life expectancy (male/female):
  69.6/73.9

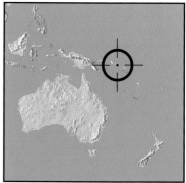

TONGA

Capital: Nuku'alofa
Area (sq km): 699
Population: 103,321 (July 2000 est)
Languages: Tongan, English
Principal religions: Christian
Currency: Pa'anga
GDP per capita (in US$): 1,788
Adult illiteracy percentage: 1%
Life expectancy (male/female):
   65.54/70.45

TUVALU

Capital: Funafuti
Area (sq km): 25
Population: 10,838 (July 2000 est)
Languages: Tuvaluan, English
Principal religions: Christian
Currency: Australian dollar
GDP per capita (in US$): 1,320
Adult illiteracy percentage: 5%
Life expectancy (male/female):
   64.21/68.53

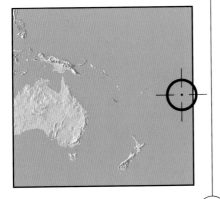

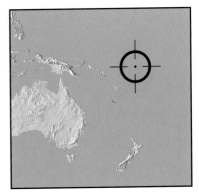

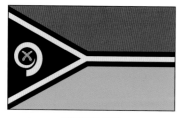

VANUATU

Capital: Port-Vila
Area (sq km): 14,765
Population: 189,618 (July 2000 est)
Languages: Bislama, English, French
Principal religions: Christian
Currency: Vatu
GDP per capita (in US$): 1,420
Adult illiteracy percentage: 33%
Life expectancy (male/female):
 59.23/61.98

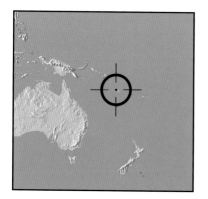

WESTERN SAMOA

Capital: Apia
Area (sq km): 2,840
Population: 179,466 (July 2000 est)
Languages: Samoan, English
Principal religions: Protestant,
 Roman Catholic
Currency: Tala
GDP per capita (in US$): 1,094
Adult illiteracy percentage: 8%
Life expectancy (male/female):
 70.66/79.84

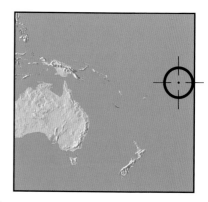

The yacht Australia II in training before its defence of the America's Cup.

INDEX

ACKNOWLEDGMENTS

All the flag images in this book, including those on the front and back covers, were supplied by Flag Institute Enterprises Ltd. The maps were created using Mountain High Maps" © 1993 Digital Wisdom, Inc. Other photographs were provided as follows:

© Duomo/CORBIS for pages 2 and 78;
Digital image © 1996 CORBIS; original image courtesy of NASA/CORBIS for page 7;
© Archivo Iconografico/CORBIS for pages 9, 10 (bottom), 35 and 40;
© Event Horizons/David Lyons for page 10 (top);
© Historical Picture Archive/CORBIS for pages 11 and 57;
© Frank Leather; Eye Ubiquitous/CORBIS for page 12;
© Danny Lehman/CORBIS for page 21;
© Neverland Ink/Trisha Collins for page 23;
© Michael Klinec for page 24;
© Charles & Josette Lenars/CORBIS for pages 27 and 30;
© Bettmann/CORBIS for pages 28, 38, 52 and 55;
© Gianni Dagli Orti/CORBIS for page 33;
© Brian Gibbs for pages 34 and 36;
© English Life Publications Ltd. for page 39. Reproduced with the kind permission of the Sulgrave Manor Board;
© Earl & Nazima Kowall/CORBIS for page 42;
© Reuters NewMedia Inc./CORBIS for pages 45 and 107;
© Paul A Souders/CORBIS for page 47;
© Wally McNamee/CORBIS for page 48;
© Mr T. M. Lucas for page 58;
© Malcolm Fife for page 60;
© TRH Pictures/US Navy for page 63;
Hulton Getty Picture Collection for page 66;
© Philip Gould/CORBIS for page 72;
© Ed Kashi/CORBIS for page 73;
© Peter Turnley/CORBIS for pages 75 and 81;
© Barnabas Bosshart/CORBIS for page 79;
© Christine Osborne/CORBIS for page 85;
© Francis G Mayer/CORBIS for page 88;
© Richard Hamilton Smith/CORBIS for page 90;
© Owen Franken/CORBIS for pages 102 and 105;
© Ron Watts/CORBIS for page 157;
Tom Wood for page 183 (right);
© Neal Preston/CORBIS for page 191 (right);
© Michael S Yamashita/CORBIS for page 217 (right);
© Adam Woolfitt/CORBIS for pages 240-241 (main);
© Roger Garwood & Trish Ainslie/CORBIS for page 253.

LIST OF FLAGS